# ESCAPING THE

# HOLLYWOOD BARDO

## Marcia Kimpton
### Director, *Bardo Blues*

*To my daughter Drennon*

# Acknowledgements

I would like to first thank my book editor Elana Freeland because without her this book would not come out of the ethers into form.

I thank my daughter Drennon for showing me unconditional love of oneself and knowing love so deep you would die for it. My daughter has been my best friend and the person who inspires me daily to be my best self. We could write another book about the journey we have taken together through the corrupt court and medical systems, but let's just say we survived. I have never met a person who handles herself with more grace, intelligence, and kindness, and I am fortunate indeed to be able to call her my daughter.

I thank my mother Louise for bringing me into this world for the miracle of life and always believing I was a superstar, even if Hollywood didn't see it. I thank my father Bill for showing me how to think outside the box and believing that one never should lower one's standards because we can always raise the bar on what is possible and do the impossible. I thank my stepfather Ray for making me laugh and providing for me, and for his honesty and integrity.

I thank my meditation teacher Gary Springfield for always listening to me and finding the answers as to how I might become more of a beam of golden light and transcend the darkness of ego. I thank Reverend Jim Lawrence for introducing me to the teachings of Emanuel Swedenborg. I thank Incho Muramatsu, or shall we say Master Tom, for teaching me Buddhism.

I thank Justin and Jason because without them I would not have my dream film. I thank my co-writer Anthony and lead actor Stephen, along with the entire cast crew in both Thailand and the U.S. who worked tirelessly to make my dream film happen. I thank my good friends Lilli and Kat for always believing in me and being there for me in my darkest days. I thank Kristen and Graham whom I miss terribly and were my biggest fans and supporters. I thank Ray, Susan, Laura and Jenny for all the lessons I learned in love and forgiveness.

Lastly, I thank my Aunt Jan who listened to me when I needed it most, and like my mother always saw the shining star I am, while the Hollywood Bardo made chasing a dream impossible.

# SPOILER ALERT

Please see the movie BARDO BLUES before reading the book because the surprise ending is given away in the first chapter. Why? Because art imitated life or life imitated art. I wrote the movie based on my brother's life and mine, and then 75% of the movie happened after I wrote it. Profound coincidence? Yes, but I can only think there must be a bigger meaning or message for the audience and readers. Otherwise, I can't fathom how these events could have overlapped...

# CONTENTS

# *Editor's Note*

Contrary to the general belief spread in the West by [Walter] Evans-Wentz, in Tibetan Buddhist practice the *Tibetan Book of Dead* is not read to the people who are passing away, but it is rather used during life by those who want to learn to visualize what will come after death.

- Paul van der Velde, Professor of Asian Religions, Radboud University Nijmegen

What is a Bardo? On an Eastern conceptual level, it's a transitional state of consciousness between past and future existence. This includes momentary states of consciousness—negative states of drunkenness, depression, rage, desire, abandonment, negligence, abuse, etc.—positive states of happiness, contentment, hope, healing, trust, etc. Bardos give us the opportunities we need in order to experience reality as it exists outside ourselves and the choice of falling or not falling into lower ego illusions, projections, deceptions, deceit, and confusion. Seeing through deception and self-deception and awakening to who we truly are—spiritual beings who have returned to the Earth to further our education as evolving beings—is the pot of gold at the end of the rainbow awaiting us all. When Ram Dass in the Sixties advised, "Be here now," he may have been trying to give us a leg up on the Bardo problem.

Basically, the *Bardo Thodol* or *Tibetan Book of the Dead* enumerates six Bardo states of consciousness, three before death and three after death. As Westerners do not like to think about death (though Western civilization has done more than its share of death-dealing), this book concentrates on the three Bardo states of consciousness familiar to us: "life" or ordinary waking consciousness, dhyana or meditation, and the dream state during sleep. These earthly Bardo states of consciousness are discussed in Liberation Through Hearing During the Intermediate State comp by Padmasambhava in the 8th century CE.

As psychoanalyst Carl Jung stressed, the emphasis that Tibetan Buddhism puts on understanding how Bardos work is not about religious ritual or dogma but about providing a map through illusion so we can concentrate on deciphering the personal and collective karmic phenomena unfolding before us by how they parallel what sleeps in our unconscious from life to life. Our dharma is inevitably to become conscious of our condition and liberate ourselves from needing to subject ourselves to the wheel of karma again and again.

Elana Freeland

# Preface

*I could always live in my art but never in my life.*

- Ingmar Bergman, *Autumn Sonata*, 1978

Did I want to be a woman warrior? No, but I was born one. My first moment of realization was at 10 years old singing Helen Reddy's 1971 revolutionary song to myself down in my dark basement, "I am woman, I am strong, I am here . . ."

Comedic stars were glowing in every living room in America: Lucille Ball, Carol Burnett, and Mary Tyler Moore. Music and TV stars helped me to escape my childhood sadness and laugh. Watching how Lucy, Carol and Mary made my mother laugh also lightened my load. I fully believed I could be a TV star when I grew up because my mother believed I could be anything I wanted to be. I didn't know any movie or TV stars, but I was determined to be one.

Nor did I know that other people were having a happy childhood. I only knew the life I was given. My mother and stepfather worked hard to give me a great education, a beautiful home, and tons of love despite our dysfunctional life in the suburbs of Chicago, which I daily yearned to escape. I wanted to be happy, I wanted to make people laugh so they would be happy.

When I was 12, I had a pivotal moment while watching Dick Clark on *American Bandstand* to escape our general family Saturday morning chaos: I suddenly knew exactly what I was going to do. My fantasy of being on TV was no longer a fantasy. I knew. I was going to have a late night rock'n'roll show with comedy. With my heroines Lucy, Carol, and Mary behind me, I could clearly see a Dick Clark, Johnny Carson Midnight Special rock'n'roll show with me as the late night emcee comedian.

What I didn't know was that women in late night didn't exist because late night was somehow a man's world. In 1986, Joan Rivers snuck her way in, but it didn't last long. Watching Lucy, Carol, and Mary (and later, Cher and Joan) made me believe there was no real reason a woman couldn't be in late night, given that funny, talented women populated TV before midnight.

Flash forward from 12 to 32 years old. I was on the Fox morning show in San Francisco doing comedy segments. Four years later on the local ABC station, I had my dream show *Live From the Starlight Room* airing at 11:30 pm on Saturday nights in a famous club from the 1920's vaudeville era. But when I tried to get a national show, every Hollywood national cable executive shook his head and said, "The world isn't ready for a woman in late night." Are women comedians that scary? I asked myself.

To prove them wrong, I would build my audience one local audience at a time. I got as far as personally driving to ten states and selling Live From the Starlight Room to 12 small TV stations. But the show was taken off the air by the ruthless new general manager (GM) who had taken over the local San Francisco ABC station, and I found myself owing my TV crew $150,000.

I am now 57 years old and writing this book to inspire others to never give up on their dreams. Sometimes while writing, I look at my Leo DiCaprio pillow given to me by my father's Kimpton Hotels Group after I asked them to promote my *Bardo Blues* film in their social media and wonder if I will manifest a script Leo loves. Maybe after he sees *Bardo Blues*, he will allow me, a woman director . . .

Despite Hollywood's well-known ageism and sexism, I have never given up on my childhood dream and have chosen instead to work my way through the Bardo states of consciousness piled up like grenades throughout Hollywood "show biz." In Hollywood terms, I am a nobody because I am not famous for a sex tape like Kim Kardashian West and her family of billionaires who say nothing, donate nothing, and change nothing on the TV landscape, except to worsen it. You may like "reality TV" and the Kardashians, but I have worked 35 years in this business trying to bring quality work to TV, and it has proven to be impossible—at least until I wrote, directed, produced, and acted in *Bardo Blues* released in theaters and digital platforms in May 2019.

I have learned that I am a somebody, even if my former power agent—who dated my best friend in high school and represented me when I was 27 at the infamous Creative Artists Agency (CAA) as his first client—now won't pick up the phone to talk to me. Being somebody means not needing Hollywood to broadcast in neon that I'm talented (though the hefty paychecks would be nice). I have found my real self and for the most part daily peace, two unquantifiables in high demand in Hollywood, despite all the money and fame that can buy just about anything else.

Isn't that the real point to a life? To have a self you stand by, and to find peace, joy and happiness beyond the success or failure of one's career? If a Bardo is a state of mind between heaven and hell, then I have made my way through the hell Hollywood metes out and found the state of mind known as creativity, and heaven in myself beyond the specifics of my childhood dream. To achieve a state of being that can create heaven wherever you live and work so you don't need the approval of the outside world, because you define your success, is to escape the illusory Bardo. How poor the Hollywood standard of money and Kardashian fame of no redeeming talent seems in comparison! I may not yet have found true love or been able to develop the career I dreamed of as a child, but I have found how to have heaven on Earth— well, most of the time.

That's my book—what I've gone through to pierce the illusions of the Hollywood Bardo and find heaven within or transcension, a word I made up to represent transcending any unfortunate experience. Circumstance forced me to find meditation and yoga so I could have heaven. Emanuel Swedenborg says the soul in the body is our internal church and all we need in order to find heaven on Earth is to reform or regenerate our self. Buddha's Eightfold Path is not only the path to compassion for others but for oneself as well, to not attach good or bad to one's journey but to observe it. This has taken years of practice, and I still catch myself being swept up in emotional dramas and bereft of observation. Even the most mundane events can drag me away, such as eating or drinking too much, or having to call AT&T for customer service.

Most moments, I AM really happy, and I don't mean as a Hollywood Bardo consolation prize. Most important has been learning how to love myself, and that it isn't dependent on anyone else or any career or family member or partner. When you love yourself and take in love and gratitude with every bite of food and everything you do, you keep your integrity and steer clear of the illusory states of mind on all sides that seek to draw you back into one Bardo or another.

***Caveat lector:*** *Given that I know some of the most powerful people in Hollywood, I have changed or deleted most of the names of the living so as not to be sued. Regarding family, the same discretion is not so much about being sued as protecting their privacy.*

# 1

# The IRS Loves Bardos

I'm at the airport when I get the call I have been waiting a month for (more like a year). It's my bookkeeper Sandy, and I am tired of listening to her smoker's voice.

"Marcia, I have good news and bad news. Which do you want first?"

"Obviously the good news. You are going to tell me I'm no longer in debt to the IRS, right?"

The shame of owing taxes creeps into every cell of my body, but my inner voice says, *Marcia, you've had no marital affairs, you don't lie, you vote, you sometimes volunteer, you help your friends, you meditate, you've given seven sermons at the Swedenborg Church and sold the most fertilizer, you were president of your high school class, and most important you were there for your daughter's every soccer, baseball, and basketball game, recital, hospital visit and graduation. You never missed an event—except for the first grade Halloween parade, which she never forgets, along with when she was in first grade and wanted you to make deviled eggs and you didn't.*

My daughter's therapist suggested she discuss these shortfalls with me, so just before her 26th birthday I had to hear it all on the phone. I replied, "I tried to make the Halloween parade, but I couldn't get out of my waitressing job. It was a small restaurant with no replacements to call. Remember my late night show got pulled off the air and I was broke, or were you too young to remember I was broke? Did I tell you that my father didn't show up for anything I did, barring one ballet recital. No graduations. Nothing. Nada."

"But Mom, what about when I brought home the eggs and you didn't make the deviled eggs?"

I ask myself, *How do you scar your child with eggs?* If this is as bad as it gets, I did a pretty great job.

All of a sudden, Sandy's smoker voice pulls me back into present time.

"Marcia, the IRS owes you $300."

I can't believe what I'm hearing. "Sandy, I can't hear you."

"Marcia, you don't owe taxes."

Can it be true? "Sandy, what's wrong with your phone line?"

Sandy coughs and coughs and finally gasps, "You're right about me needing a new phone."

Meanwhile I'm thinking, What you really need is to stop smoking two packs a day. But I can't save her from lung cancer. Maybe her mother smoked, and I bet her husband and grandfather do to this day. I can't tell her anything because I don't know her and I don't want to know her. She is the bookkeeper that I want to replace but can't afford to because I owe money to the IRS. Damn. So I try harder to hear her and believe what I'm hearing.

"Sandy, are you saying I don't owe the IRS?"

"Yes."

I get up and start dancing in the Nice airport, throwing my hands up in the air. People stare because radiating joy is forbidden at airports. Only sullen or stressed faces are allowed (unless you're boarding a plane to Hawaii). I want to scream, but since 9/11 you can't scream at the airport, either.

You know what else you can't do since 9/11? As I prepared to board the plane, they asked, "Does anyone need help?" I raised my hand and said, "Yes, I desperately need help because I have a terrible hangover." It was a joke, but it didn't go over well. In fact, the steward wouldn't let me board, even though I begged and begged. Finally, 15 minutes after everyone had boarded and they were closing the door, he let me on. I had thought I was being funny, but I found out post-9/11 airlines don't have the same sense of humor as I do, nor does the IRS.

Back to my moment of happiness with Sandy before boarding my plane.

"Thank you, Sandy. I love you, Sandy. So for 2017, I owe no taxes, and all my expenses for making the film canceled out my IRS back taxes?"

"I didn't say that, Marcia."

"Sandy, is this back to your phone line not working, or am I going deaf due to the 1,232 concerts I've attended over the last three decades, including Pearl Jam, Rolling Stones, Who, Black Crows, Florence and the Machine, Lauryn Hill, etc.?"

"Marcia, I said you don't owe any taxes with your production company because we both know you didn't make any money, which was why I was wondering why you were so excited."

"I swear you said I don't owe the IRS, or is it Alzheimer's and not loss of hearing?"

"I said you don't owe the IRS for your company and likely not for your personal taxes for 2017, but I haven't finished them so I can't be sure."

I'm thinking, *Well, gee, Sandy, what the fuck have you been doing in Florida? Drinking piña coladas at the Jimmy Buffet oceanfront bar where most Floridian drunks show up by noon? Because when you tell someone who owes a tax lien that they don't owe the IRS . . .*

I exercise self-restraint. "Sandy, when will I know if I owe for 2017? It's causing me sleepless nights, and I can't do Ambien again because I am pretty sure they are now outsourcing it to China and mixing it with chemicals. You don't want me feeling suicidal, do you? Now, when I take

Ambien, I want to jump off the Brooklyn Bridge. When I was addicted to Ambien five years ago after my trip to India, I was only getting over jet lag and didn't feel suicidal. Granted, President Trump wasn't yet in office . . . Oh, I'm sorry, Sandy, maybe you're a Republican like many people in Florida." My parents used to be Republicans.

OK, that's a run-on paragraph, but my mind doesn't have periods and commas when it is thinking. I'm like James Joyce thinking and writing in stream of consciousness tense.

Of course, I don't tell Sandy that it's really her who is causing me sleepless nights. I have done enough spiritual retreats to India, Bhutan, and Santa Cruz to realize I create the problem, not Sandy, though I do wish she had created the problem so I could blame her. But I have awakened to the idea that we are responsible for our reality and it is me who hasn't broken through the emotional childhood wound of feeling I am incapable of making, handling, and saving money. Had I healed that wound, I am sure I wouldn't have a tax lien and would be making millions of dollars with my movies, despite the low odds of female filmmakers getting any work in Hollywood. Only five women have been nominated for best director since the Oscars began in 1929, and only one woman has won. Because I want to be nominated, I suppose I must thank the fucking IRS for forcing me to look deep inside to consider the wound that still needs healing, so I will put the dozens of IRS tax lien reminders on my spiritual altar and petition them to care about woman filmmakers.

Instead of telling Sandy all of this, I say nicely through my gnashing of teeth, "When you said 'Marcia, you don't owe taxes,' I foolishly thought I was hearing that I don't owe taxes and am debt free!"

"Marcia, I'm sorry if I miscommunicated, but you should be happy that your production company doesn't owe taxes."

I want to scream, "I could have figured that out on my own because you can't owe taxes if you don't make money!"

Instead, I hold my breath and count to five, then let it out on another five-count, reciting in my mind, *I want to reach enlightenment in this lifetime even if I think it is unlikely,* recalling what my meditation teacher promised: "Marcia, each step forward in kindness, patience and love moves you towards enlightenment." I am an adult, right?

I calmly say, "Sandy, let's go over this again so I understand you clearly. My company doesn't owe money and I likely won't owe money because of my huge expenses in making the movie in 2017. But I still owe the IRS $250,000, don't I?"

"Yes, Marcia."

"So I can't use the $200,000 in film expenses last year towards the past tax debt like I did for 2012, 2013 and 2014?"

Sandy says nothing.

"Now you're sure about that, Sandy?"

"That's the law, Marcia. Can't get around it."

I want to track an IRS agent down for a brutal, long, torturous murder. I am now discovering my really dark side. I will cut each of his limbs off while screaming at him, "Why do you not allow a woman filmmaker a break on her taxes and let her, me, take all film expenses as deductions? Why? Why not? Do you know only 4 percent of women get to direct films?"

Then the IRS agent screams back, "We're not in the business of investing in film!" He has a point, but I've risked everything for this film, even my taxes.

I counter. "And before I cut off your second arm, you had better tell me why only one woman, specifically Kathryn Bigelow, won best director."

My fantasy IRS agent is silent.

"And let me add, as I slowly cut off each of your toes, that she had to make a film about men in war risking their lives to detonate bombs in order to win. Why aren't women's stories ever recognized?"

My knife flashes and another toe is gone.

"Let's talk about my movie *Bardo Blues* and how I have no shot at getting it nominated unless I have a million dollars for promotion."

Another bloody toe rolls into the corner.

From a great distance, I hear raspy Sandy. "Marcia, are you there? I really need to get off the phone to work on your personal taxes so we can file in time. I don't want you to get any more penalties."

"Thank you, Sandy, but can you tell me why we can't deduct film expenses from 2015 and 2016?"

"Marcia, we did that for your other $200,000 in back taxes, when you owed $450,000, and then remember how the law changed?"

"Why did the law change? To give the IRS more of our money so they can use it for corrupt practices?"

"I agree with you that government seems useless . . ."

The headless, nameless IRS agent in my mind loses another toe and screams in pain.

I tune back into Sandy's deathbed voice. ". . . so they think people are avoiding paying taxes with the Subchapter S corporation[1]."

I don't care about tax laws except when they change my future, particularly when it comes to having enough money to nominate myself for an Oscar because no one else will. My film may not be Oscar-worthy, but I have seen many nominated films not as good as mine, so I want an Oscar nomination. I worked 35 years toward this goal, and I may be dreaming too big, but that's how dreams happen, isn't it? So my taxes equate to helping or hindering an Oscar nomination.

---

[1] Subchapter S is a form of corporation that meets specific Internal Revenue Code requirements giving a corporation with 100 shareholders or fewer the benefit of incorporation while being taxed as a partnership. The corporation may pass income directly to shareholders and avoid double taxation. Requirements include being a domestic corporation, not having more than 100 shareholders, including only eligible shareholders, and having only one class of stock. – *Investopedia*

Sandy is my road to an Oscar, but all she knows is that she is the road to the IRS not taking away my car and house because I have no savings because every dime I have has gone into my art. In the history of woman filmmaking, has any other woman gone down this road? But I've always wanted to make history. I just didn't think my history would include the IRS filing a lien against me.

"Marcia, you can't get around the $55,000 in interest incurred for not paying your taxes."

I think to myself that a 2 percent loan on my money is better than going to the bank that wasn't going to give me that big of a loan to do my movie. Not paying my taxes was worth having made my dream movie, but was the unbearable anxiety? The IRS had invested in my film without knowing it, and then all of a sudden they wanted their money back. There appeared to be no way of convincing them differently.

"Can't I just not pay the lien? They saw me pay $13,000 monthly for a year. They know I will pay one day again, right?"

"Marcia, you have to pay your taxes. Everyone has to pay their taxes. You know. Death and taxes."

"But what can they do? I have nothing but an old BMW. Let them take away my house. I don't own it anyway!"

I always paid my taxes on time and am not stupid. You can't avoid taxes like you can't avoid death. The history of the IRS is rife with corruption, and the banks and government were in on it. I once thought taxes were to help the poor and to build bridges and highways, but it turns out that the real truth was straight out of conspiracy theories. Taxes were more like mob protection rackets.

"Sandy, I know I have to pay, but the question is when. If I don't have a theatrical release for my film, which alone costs around $100,000, I won't qualify for the Oscars. I cannot just put *Bardo Blues* up on iTunes. No one buys movies on iTunes, but then again no one goes to the movie theater, so if I am not on Netflix or Amazon, I am fucked. Fortunately, I have

Bill Vergos at Freestyle selling it, but I must be in the movie theaters in order to qualify for the Oscars, Sandy! I want an Oscar nomination even if my film isn't *The Godfather*. If I had done everything right by the IRS, I wouldn't have *Bardo Blues*, so I'm glad I did the wrong thing—aren't I?"

I briefly contemplated the possibility that doing the wrong thing could actually be the right thing, then realized that I had moved from kvetching to Sandy into begging and wallowing. A big sigh escaped from me.

"Sandy, this film is about my 48-year-old brother who died without seeing it . . ."

*I feel myself heading down the slippery slope of memory to the call from my stepsister Jenny who never calls me, the call I had feared for decades.*

*"Is everything OK, Jenny?"*

*"No."*

*"Is Graham OK?"*

*"No."*

*"Graham isn't dead," I said dully, as if saying it would make it true.*

*"He is."*

*I fall to my knees in the parking lot of a Travelodge in Torrance, California, the worst hotel in Los Angeles County I'd been able to find, for the last scene of Bardo Blues. Nine of us are crammed into a bleak Travelodge room filled with empty beer cans we collected the night before. I'd purposely written the film for Graham after he'd talked about suicide as his only way out of the suffering he had undergone for over 20 years.*

*My brother hadn't read the script.*

*I'm directing the scene of Jack's suicide just hours after my brother has committed suicide, but I don't know it yet. When I get the call, I have just asked the room to be quiet and respectful of Stephen McClintic playing Jack who is at that moment lying on the bed, scrolling through his mind for his*

26

*saddest memory. I say, "Action!" and direct him to think about suicide. "Pick up the beer can and drink." (It's water.) "Get up and open the curtain. This is your last day, the last moment of life."*

*He turns his head at an angle. His bone structure, sadness and look are all my brother's. I have a strange feeling.*

*"It's that bad, Stephen. Your only alternative is to choose to die."*

*Once the scene is a wrap, we have just one more shot for the* **SPOILER ALERT** *gracefully showing the suicide without showing it.*

*"How should we do it?" I ask my cameraman Justin McAleece. I don't want to show anything but the rope, but how can we do it tastefully?*

*The room is hot and stuffy. Justin walks back and forth, thinking, then closes the bathroom door. We open the hall door for more air.*

*My assistant walks in to say that my mother keeps calling and other family members keep texting. I look at my texts and see Jenny's:* Please call me its important. Many missed calls from her. *She'd texted me earlier to ask if I had heard from Graham.* No, *I'd texted, while driving to the Travelodge.*

*That's when I got the call. The death of my best friend, my brother I could not save. Helplessness and powerlessness, one more time. Feeling powerless always makes me want to leave wherever I am. I have this same feeling now as I write. I can't escape, but I can shut it all down and hide it in the corners of trauma until another lifetime, or until someone triggers the wounds thus far unhealed . . .*

Suddenly, Sandy intrudes. "Marcia, I really need to get off the phone to file your taxes."

I can barely hear her, my thought stream is so insistent.

*The word* panic *is from Pan, the Greek god of the wild who used to cause unreasonable fear in humans so they would flee.*

*The week before while location scouting, I'd called a mortuary owner to see if we could film in the funeral home, but he'd refused. He didn't want us to film there because of the public's sensitivity to death, so we'd filmed a mortuary owner character in the car saying to the lead character, Jack, "When are you going to pick up the body?"—exactly what my stepmother was asked to do for Graham's body within a few hours of filming that scene. She had to make arrangements for the funeral home to pick up his body from his artist loft. By the grace of God, Graham had double locked his loft. Thus it was the police and not Graham's mother who found his body hanging off the pool table surrounded by his brilliant artwork.*

*I regret not asking to see Graham's body. I so badly wanted to see him one last time in the flesh. My stepsister said it was his body, but Graham wasn't in it anymore. I didn't see my father after he died, either. I have never seen a dead person. As Swedenborg said, the soul is all that animates the body.*

*I drove from LA to San Francisco to grieve with my family, but not one family member came to see me in the three days I spent meditating in Graham's house and artist loft. The trauma was too much. No one could mourn together until three months later.*

From far away, Sandy's softened voice draws me back. "I'm sorry about your brother, Marcia. I didn't even know you had a brother."

I continued speaking as if I hadn't just vanished. ". . . We were just trying to figure out a delicate way to show the suicide, and I got the call that my brother had hung himself."

"Oh, Marcia . . ."

"I know you don't know what to say, Sandy. No one does, really. It was awful. He was my best friend and sole

28

investor, and he never got to see it. I really wanted him to see it
. . ."

*Graham's $50,000 investment had come at a crucial moment. I had stopped paying my taxes a few years before, thinking I had enough to do the film, but I didn't. Making a low budget indie film is expensive if you are personally paying for everything. A woman director/filmmaker without a successful track record trying to find investors in Hollywood or anywhere is basically impossible. My brother knew that and that his investment would make it possible for us to shoot in Thailand when it wasn't so hot.*

*One night en route to Thailand, I drove from Los Angeles to San Francisco to drop off my dogs with my dog sitter and have dinner with Graham. I told him I was on my way to Northern Thailand to do casting and location shooting but was concerned that I didn't have enough money and that I would likely have to postpone production for a year because of the heat.*

*"How much do you need to shoot this year?" Graham asked.*

*"$50,000."*

*"Where should I send a check?"*

*It was that simple. I had never really had that kind of support from any man in my life. My brother loved and supported me and had helped me creatively on so many projects. The check arrived, and we shot the film in 16 days in February 2016. I'd invited him to Thailand, but his difficult mental inner world would not allow a long flight and a foreign country.*

*He saved the day for me one last time. I had called him and said I would love to give the cast and crew a wrap party but was $5,000 off. He sent the check to my daughter, who transferred it to my account so I wouldn't leave Thailand without paying my bill. I had been late on bills but never not* *paid a bill, especially a hotel bill. Once again, I'd done the numbers wrong.*

A sigh from Sandy over the telephone brought me back to tax reality. I could tell that she didn't know what to say. Maybe no client had ever told her such a story of loss, on top of which she didn't want to tell me not to pay my taxes. As a bookkeeper, she strove for the balanced books path, but I was a moviemaker, an illusion-generator, a fantasist. Sandy was the kind of bookkeeper one wants to have keeping tabs on one's money, who does everything to the letter, by the book, the exception being the one to two packs a day she smoked. But how could I who make movies and live by my imagination judge her? If I had her job, I would smoke every waking hour. High consumption of tobacco could just as well mean her husband is bad in bed and they stopped having sex twenty years ago. Her smoking may have nothing to do with bookkeeping. Who knows? You can think anything you want in your mind, and it's a wild and crazy world in the mind of Marcia.

Sandy's raspy voice summons me. "Marcia, I can't tell anyone to not pay their taxes, but I would love to see your film."

"My brother supported me more than anyone, Sandy. He'd never read the script of *Bardo Blues* and yet hung himself in his artist loft within 24 hours of my filming the suicide scene. I wish I knew what that means . . ."

Sandy was hesitant. "You're not saying he wanted to—support you—with his—?" Sandy couldn't say the word.

In my astrology reading by Gael Sasson I'd learned that the dead, by their death, may bequeath a gift that often appears as a coincidence, like my shooting the last *Bardo Blues* scene while Graham was . . . Gael's reading gave me solace. He also said that my chart revealed a lot of transformation through death. When my grandmother died, she was 48 and I was one; my father died at 65 when I was 39; my brother died at 48 when I was 54; and the year before his death, my daughter died in my arms and came back to life at the age of 23. Add to this that I hear from the dead on a regular basis, like it or not.

I asked Gael to clarify the transformation through death thing. He said that whatever death may mean in the lives of others, it impacts me through my consciousness. For example, letting go of my brother or even permanently letting go of a thought process will produce a death and transformation in my consciousness. Letting go of the past is how we truly move on to greater consciousness.

"I know it sounds strange, Sandy, but how else can I come to grips with such a synchronicity of events except by acknowledging that my brother wanted me to tell his story? I made the film for him to see, and prevent the inevitability of his suicide." I laugh darkly, "Obviously, that didn't happen."

"Again, I am so sorry, Marcia."

I could hear myself still talking and laughing. "Graham had a wicked sense of humor and would have wanted me to find the humor in his tragedy. He was a brilliant artist battling the voices of schizophrenia, possibly the voices of the dead. Have you ever heard of that interpretation of schizophrenia?"

"No."

"Wilson Van Dusen, a psychologist who studied the ideas of the 19th century phenomenologist Emanuel Swedenborg, cured 25 out of 100 schizophrenics at Mendocino State Hospital by having them talk to the dead or spirits they were hearing in their heads. I met Van Dusen when I was studying Swedenborg at the Pacific School of Religion. Unfortunately, my brother's psychiatrist was not a Dr. Van Dusen. Graham's West Coast psychiatrist at UCSF had been kind and smart, whereas his East Coast McLean psychiatrist was old school and brutal. A few years before Graham, one of his patients had jumped to his death from a building in Cambridge Square near Harvard Medical School. I asked my brother, 'Why are you seeing this psychiatrist, even if he is part of the revered McLean Hospital?' Graham said he liked the challenge of outsmarting the McLean doctor who only knew how to prescribe pills. Before his death, Graham did have a wonderful woman doctor, but no one came close to Dr. Van Dusen's insights.— Sandy, have you ever talked to the dead?"

I sensed that Sandy was looking for a convenient escape from an increasingly bizarre conversation.

"No, nor have I tried, but—"

"I believe we can, and I have heard from the dead—but that's a whole other conversation, and we were talking about my taxes, weren't we, Marcia?"

"Yes, taxes," Sandy said, relieved.

But I wasn't quite ready to stop. "My brother fought for his sanity for 25 years, Sandy."

"So hard, Marcia . . ."

". . . hard and heartbreaking for our family because he was so special. Movie star looks, cutting-edge artist who made you laugh . . . By the time Graham jumped off the pool table and hung himself, he had moved on to a much better therapist who tried her hardest and told me so when I met her at the memorial. I told Graham his previous psychiatrist (then retired) should be jailed. But Graham's family did nothing about it, nor was I ever asked for my opinion. My father was dead, and I was no longer recognized as a family member. I have no idea if I could have helped. Maybe it was just fate, destiny, and no one could have saved Graham but himself, I have no idea . . ."

I needed to pull out of this backward slope of memory and contemplation of death and transformation.

"He sounds special," Sandy backpedaled, looking for her own way off my backward slope.

"He was. But all the doctors did was give him tons of meds in the name of helping him. I can't prove that the drugs contributed to my brother losing all his dopamine, but I believe they did. Do you know what dopamine does, Sandy?"

"No."

"It is the chemical that along with serotonin keeps you happy. My brother was prescribed dextroamphetamines, a fun drug if you don't have a mental illness, but if you do, it fucks with your brain . . ."

I found out later that dextroamphetamine and amphetamine go by the brand name Adderall. With a bunch of margaritas, it's a killer high but dangerous. I watched my brother do it for years and then tried it with him at a mansion party on the Atlantic coast, just after dropping my daughter off at her boarding school. Graham understood that I wouldn't be seeing her until a court-ordered parent weekend, so when he offered it, I said, "What the fuck, hand me a few." Did Graham help me in my hour of need? Yes. Do drugs help in the long run? No, and in the case of drugs prescribed by doctors— doctors more than willing to prescribe drugs for kickbacks from the drug companies—there are always side effects. At best, all drugs are a temporary fix.

I continued explaining to Sandy. "Dextro feels like speed but better, and yet not as good as cocaine, the devil of all drugs because the high leads to hell. Eventually, dextro kills the brain's dopamine or serotonin and you become depressed and then want to kill yourself. Dextro made it worse for Graham in the end.—What do you think, Sandy? Should my brother have taken the drug that may have led to his suicide?"

"I don't take drugs, so I wouldn't know," Sandy said.

"Half of America is on antidepressants. I finally went on dextro . . ."

"You did?"

"I got a prescription for it. I know we should do my taxes, but I need to tell you the dextro story. My ex-husband hired a powerful lawyer when my 12-year-old daughter wanted to live full-time with me. Thanks to dickhead—sorry, I shouldn't refer to him like that—we were stuck in the California court system for over a year and a half and $400,000 in legal fees—who doesn't want to help lawyers out, right?— until the evaluator the court had appointed took my daughter away from me."

"What? How is that possible?"

"A woman who does past life regressions told me that I must have given the order to cut off the heads of both the evaluator and my ex-husband back in the 17th century when I was the first Queen Elizabeth and this was my karmic payback in the 21st century. Of course, no one can prove it, so I have to just accept the facts of my current life: my daughter court-ordered to an East Coast boarding school and me with only one visit per semester and one phone call per week, all based on my karma. I can't even visit her on her birthday."

"What can I say, Marcia?"

"Well, that's why I ended up on dextro. The court evaluator said I was depressed and she was right. Who wouldn't be when your ex-husband takes your child away? The court evaluator ordered me to see a psychiatrist and suggested I be on medication due to the psychiatrist's Rorschach inkblot interpretation. Rorschach tests should be banned from court evaluations, but I don't have time to take on that fight. I'm fighting for women directors' Oscar nominations."

"'Rorschach test'? I never heard of it, Marcia."

"Look it up. It's a bunch of stupid inkblot shapes on a page that tell the psychiatrist if you are depressed or psychotic or lonely or whatever. We are all of that at one point or another, aren't we, Sandy? In fact, that's life, or at least that's my life." I was on a roll. "That inkblot evaluator should be in jail and not allowed to practice. But there are no victims, right, Sandy?"

"Right!" This was the first time I actually heard Sandy's raspy voice loud and clear.

"And doctors are more than willing to prescribe drugs for the kickbacks they get from the drug companies. That's how I ended up on dextroamphetamine."

"I've never done drugs," Sandy repeated, desperate for some nicotine before tackling my taxes.

"Good, Sandy, because people in pain hope drugs will take the pain away, and they do, for few days, but in the end you are only worse off. Believe me, I've tried enough to know.

Miraculously, I've never been a drug addict, except maybe for grass. In fact, I thank grass for helping me get through my hellish upbringing and divorce, but now it's dumbing down all of America. I was all for legalizing drugs, but now people are just stupid." I stared at the phone. "What do you think, Sandy?"

"I don't know, I haven't noticed that people are any stupider than usual."

"And of course there is always an upside to everything. Guess what the upside is for dextro?"

"What?"

"On dextro, I could sit and read for six hours straight, despite being ADD. I was in a master's program studying Swedenborg at the Pacific School of Religion with 600 pages per week to read. It was magic in the brain! But after six weeks I was throwing it down the toilet. You're not supposed to know that, but I was afraid I would find it in the garbage the next day and take more."

"Why did you throw it away?"

"I became suicidal and was drinking more and more alcohol because the dextro high was too alert, too hyper. I drank an entire bottle of tequila, then wondered why my daughter had been sent away and why my late night show had been taken off the air. After passing out, I was awakened by Frank, my friend Neka's father who had just died. Frank said to me, "Wake up! You are dying." That was the last time I took those dangerous pills. I then had to sit in the pain of knowing that I couldn't be with my daughter until I sobered up, which I then did."

"I'm glad you got off the drugs," Sandy said, not noticing that I'd referred to being saved by someone who was dead.

Sandy was obviously my new friend and therapist. I need a therapist but can't afford one.

"Sorry, Sandy, I've gotten a little off course, especially if I'm regurgitating my dextro-almost-dying story. The point is,

I don't want to pay my taxes until I get the Oscar nomination. Let them chase me with the lien as I chase the Oscars."

"But Marcia, you've been paying the lien all this year. Why stop?"

"I'm supposed to pay because they put the fear of God in me?"

"No, you are supposed to pay because it's the law."

"I'll pay, but I want to pay on my terms. I finally feel fearless." Actually, I felt a bit like Thelma and Louise going off the cliff.

"But you can't get around the IRS," Sandy reminded. (Death and taxes.)

"I know, but if I hadn't risked everything, I wouldn't have made *Bardo Blues*. What do you think I did, Sandy?"

"I have no idea, but I feel bad saying we really need to figure out if you are going to continue with your installment agreement."

"We will, Sandy. Just hear me out a bit more because you are helping me make the decision of paying my taxes or not."

"OK, I'm glad I'm helping."

What Sandy meant is that after all this heavy info she has to get off the phone and smoke a cig. It was more than she could handle without nicotine, but I needed to figure out if I was going for the Oscar or paying the tax lien that could track me down and make it impossible for me to get the Oscar nomination.

"So what do you think I did when I ran out of money, back when my brother was still alive?"

"I don't know."

"I pushed back finishing the film twice because I kept thinking I could afford to film the last 3 days in LA but not until June 12, 13, 14. So the last scene, the last moment of filming in that terrible Travelodge is when I get the call. Why? We changed the dates twice, my brother hadn't read the script and didn't know we were filming that day . . ."

36

I paused. Strangely enough, I had texted everyone I knew about the car crash scene, but had forgotten my brother on his last night alive. It suddenly occurred to me that if I'd had the money, I wouldn't have postponed finishing the film. What would that have meant for Graham?

Sandy needed a cigarette, but she was riveted.

Numbly, I went on. "The movie was to prevent his suicide, but I changed the dates twice. Can you believe that, Sandy?"

I thought about Swedenborg who says we never die, we just change form. My brother didn't believe we go anywhere after death. How was he seeing things now?

Sandy made the decision I couldn't. "I'll call the IRS tomorrow and get back to you."

I felt immediate relief. Thelma and Louise's cliff remained for another day. "Thank you, Sandy. Feel free to tell them my story." I knew she wouldn't.

"They usually just cut me off and don't care what I have to say," she said glumly.

"Because it's all about money, right, always about money?" I tried to imagine a job in which every day you eventually have to talk to the IRS.

The next day I didn't hear from her. All day I was nervous. By the next day, I'm thinking maybe she was off having an affair behind her husband's back and got caught, and the last thing she can do is think about my taxes as she watches her marriage crumble. I wait until the next day to call, hoping everything I fantasized in the crazy world of Marcia's mind has blown over.

She picks up.

"Sandy, it's been three days since we talked, and I was just wondering if you reached the IRS?"

"I did."

"And you didn't call me? Is everything OK?"

"Everything is fine and normal. I proposed a lower payment plan and was going to call you once it is approved."

"If it is approved. So why haven't they called you back?"

Is no news from the IRS good news?

"It's April 12 and I'm sure they are very busy. I had to wait two hours on the phone for someone to answer."

"I'm so sorry you had to wait so long. What did they say after the two hours?"

"I had to hang up."

"Hang up? Why?"

"I've been doing this for 30 years, Marcia, and I know all the different units in this huge bureaucracy. Once I recognized the voice of the IRS agent I knew wouldn't approve lower payments, I hung up and tried again today, only to get the same agent."

"You hung up the phone for me! Wow, Sandy, you're amazing. It restores my faith in humankind as our government is taking us to hell in a hand basket."

"It was the least I could do after hearing your story."

"I'll hang in there with you, Sandy. I know I'm in good hands."

She called a week later and said she got me an installment agreement down from $13,000 to $4,000 just because she waited for the right agent. He still didn't think the IRS should invest in women's films, but he said I could pay it slower at more interest. I didn't care. Sandy is my BFF.

Bardo after Bardo, and then into heaven!

# 2

# Dancing Next to Jennifer Aniston

The bed swishes back and forth like I am floating on the ocean but it's different when someone is on top of you. Steve is 6 foot 6, gorgeous, introverted, and funny. I met him in 1996 at a New Year's Eve party in Aspen, only to find out he lived three blocks from me in San Francisco. I enjoyed his water bed, but he was one of those short-term relationships that you think in the beginning could be long term but it's all really based on him being tall, gorgeous, funny and nice and about passing the dating test of 3 weeks, then 6 weeks, hoping for 3 months, and if you make it past the 6 month mark you are golden. But we didn't. Fortunately, it was mutual and my heart was broken again like with the love of my life from Denmark. Like my Viking, my SF man and I had a nice beginning, but aren't all relationships nice in the beginning?

That New Year's Eve we danced the night away on the dance floor at the Hotel Jerome, a famous 1889 Old West silver boom building on Main Street in Aspen. What made it particularly memorable was that we were dancing right next to Jennifer Aniston, who was so unobvious until she became obvious by toasting her new fame on *Friends*. At least I thought that was what she was toasting because that is what I would be doing if I had a hit TV series after years of trying. She was 26 years old and I was 34 years old, and technically I had only been trying for seven years. She hadn't gone to college like I had; she had gone straight into acting.

As I reflect on Jennifer that night 22 years ago, I realize I was psychologically projecting my New Year's Eve toast onto her, something I have done all my life with many "successful" people—an unconscious defense mechanism in order to cope with difficult feelings or emotions rather than admitting to myself that I too want a comedy TV series like Jennifer Aniston's. You can call it jealousy but I wasn't exactly jealous; I was happy for her. It was the ego inside my head that wanted to be making that same exact toast that night about my hit TV series that still hasn't happened—the dream I will not give up on until I am deep in the ground with the worms.

And I assume that as Jennifer was making her toasts that New Year's Eve, she never imagined she would marry Brad Pitt because that would have been a hell of a toast, given that no one really thinks they could ever marry Brad Pitt. They only dream of marrying him.

Am I projecting again? Do I need a therapy session in order to finish this chapter? No. I have been single for years because I have learned to love myself and don't need a Brad Pitt to love me in order to be complete, despite my fantasy life. How far I've come! Loving yourself and not waiting for some man to do it for you is the most important, with or without a Brad Pitt.

So Jennifer did make that wedding toast a few years later, and if I may indulge myself one more time, she probably said something like, "I am the luckiest woman in the world to find love with the most handsome, talented, and kind man," and Brad said something like my ex-husband who thought he had found true love, "I am the luckiest man in the world to find a woman like you. You are so funny, humble, and beautiful."

Come on, Marcia, I thought you just told us that Brad Pitt means nothing if you love yourself? And did they say that on their wedding day? And how do you know he's the kindest man on Earth? Really, I mean at the end of the day Brad Pitt, like Mick Jagger, is still just a human being, despite movie star looks and talent. More importantly, why should anyone other than them really care? Yes, I want to make people laugh like Jennifer does, and I want to marry Brad Pitt like she did, despite a divorce. Millions have watched her comedy, whereas only 232 have viewed my *Planet M* web series and 8,212 my *An American in Amsterdam*. But who's counting? To continue comparing myself with Jennifer Aniston (which no one who loves herself should do), I have to add how long I have been single and incapable of making money with my art. Ten million watched the final episode of *Friends*. On the other hand, my first marriage lasted as long as hers, and I was fortunate enough to have a beautiful daughter, though no TV series.

Flash-forward from New Year's Eve in Aspen to 20 years later and I am still pitching my *Planet M* and *An American in Amsterdam* for a TV series to anyone who will listen and has money to pay for the production. (You know how seriously in debt I am to the IRS.) Why with talent but no lucky breaks like Jennifer Aniston I have to put up my own personal money in order to see my art realized is something I still resist. Is it sexism, or just bad luck or karma, aka Fate? When I hear gurus say we manifest our reality, why is it so difficult to sell these comedy shows with the plethora of crap out there on TV? And Brad Pitt is now single again, but I no longer want to marry him, not because he isn't an amazing, gorgeous movie star putting out amazing, thought-provoking movies like *The Big Short*, but because I just don't. I'd take a date with him, though.

Funny how life works out. I now dream differently than when I was dancing next to Jennifer because I am happy today. Back then, I was unhappy with the sexist GM I talk about later in the book who put me and my comedic segments on the morning FOX show once a week for two minutes for the bargain basement cost of $150 because I wouldn't sleep with him. My brother Graham helped me with each comedic segment I slaved at editing on VHS and Beta deck by coming over to my San Francisco apartment to help me find the comedy in each segment.

The TV biz also means that someone hungry for fame and money is waiting in the wings to take your job at a moment's notice. Ryan Seacrest was right there, and did. My assistant found him on radio and suggested to him that he be on TV, and the next thing I knew, I was no longer called for entertainment subbing and Ryan was in my spot. Within a year or two, he was negotiating a $20 million contract with ABC for the next season of *American Idol*.

For the record, Ryan wasn't trying to take my job. It just happened because he was male. There's no other way around it. I was talented and very good on camera, to the confusion of the head *Morning* host who took me out to lunch and said, "I just don't understand why you aren't going further at this station . . ." At the time, I didn't really realize that the woman ex-producer was jealous from looking at me on camera, plus I wouldn't sleep with the GM. Therefore, Ryan Seacrest gets ahead and I'm still on for two minutes a week with a pay raise of $100, making a whopping total of $250 per week.

Finding the elusive happiness drug is not easy. I looked for a long time in bottles of Chardonnay and a short time in drugs, and came up empty-handed. (Psilocybin mushrooms did expand my consciousness, but given that they ruin your kidneys, I opted to only take them every ten years.) Granted, it's a lot of work finding and funding happiness on our own without Big Pharma or psychotropic help, but being unhappy is more work in the long run, and more expensive, don't you think? I've meditated in temples in Bhutan, India, Thailand and Laos—years of traveling to meet every healer possible, with diet, meditation, contemplation, analysis, and yoga clues that could lead to a spiritually content Marcia. I had the laughter piece of the Bardo puzzle—if we can't laugh at ourselves, then crying or not feeling at all may be all that is left—but I needed the rest. This is what chapter 8 is about.

Jennifer Aniston was symbolic of the state of mind I was in during my thirties. I admired her that night while dancing next to her in Aspen because she is a great comedic actress. I still admire her because she is a great all-around actress who just produced a lovely film called *Dumplin'*. She has handled herself beautifully in the Hollywood Bardo, maybe even attaining Hollywood heaven—and I don't mean the millions of dollars, even if does make life financially easier. No one really knows how hard it is to do comedy until you do it. (I also admire Supreme Court Justice Ruth Ginsburg, Gloria Steinem, and Maya Angelou, so it's not like I am just a star fucker.)

I always thought I would be famous, but why do I need to be famous? When I was dancing next to Jennifer, I wanted to be famous to gain power, money, and great artistic jobs so my father would finally recognize and respect me. What has changed since that New Year's Eve, besides a few more pounds and wrinkles (if I don't Botox them away or put stem cells on my face, thanks to the Carole Maggio Spa in LA), is I actually have an inner life now.

Had I become as famous as I then dreamed, would I have found as much internal peace, or would I be stroking my ego with famous friends, tons of money and creative opportunities? It would have made the me in my thirties happy, but would it have been real happiness, especially as I aged?

Jane Fonda, whom I admire for acting, producing great movies, and activism, appeared happy in her glamorous Hollywood life but later revealed that until she turned 60 and did her life review, she'd never been happy. So had I become as famous as I dreamed, I would perhaps have a full-time assistant to help my one-woman production company, but I also might have become dependent upon Leo DiCaprio calling me or not calling me to work on a 20th Century Fox Martin Scorsese (one of my favorite directors) gratuitous violence film starring opposite Sean Penn or Jack Nicholson (my dream actors to work with). It would have allowed me to donate to

Leo's important Stop Global Warming fund, and I would have felt happy about that, but would I have been happy? Of course, if I had been working with Leo, Mary, Sean, Jack, Meryl, or Charlize, I would have, but my happiness would probably have been contingent upon the next movie doing well or not, or the next person I would work with. Hollywood is a roller coaster until you get out of the rich-and-famous Bardo mold and see and feel what real life is really about.

Is it because I am a qualified, talented woman rejected over and over and with zero luck that I turn to fantasizing scenarios like this? I've figured out ways to write, produce without an assistant, direct and act in a low budget film that has gotten over 15 awards from small film festivals, but still find myself dreaming about top talent reading my scripts and me directing them. If I were to pitch my Big Pharma corruption script to Leo or Brad, would he love it and consider me as the director? An agent dropped me in my twenties and another in my thirties. If in my fifties *Bardo Blues* is a hit, I just might be able to get my third agent and even Leo's attention. If it isn't a hit, I'll still be in debt and scrambling for my next production.

In Hollywood, the fact is that women directors are not asked, not nominated, and basically have to fight tooth and high-gloss nail to get a film made, not to mention that naming the Big Pharma company that has committed crimes for which they are still settling 30 years later will mean a gun to my head.[2] While trying to sell the Big Pharma script Brian Goss and I wrote, I piqued the interest of a top CAA agent representing a huge female star who might be interested in playing the lead role. When he asked who was directing and I responded with my name, I heard nothing more.

I can hear the PR agent I hired to promote *Bardo Blues* humbling me now with how no one will want to write an article about me because I haven't managed to get into

---

[2] Speaking of which, Jane Fonda recently emailed me that her agent is now trying to help me sell my Big Pharma exposé script.

Sundance, Tribeca, Telluride or Toronto. I respond that I've tried, but the truth is that if an agent isn't pushing hard to get you into the festival, forget it because it has nothing to do with your film or artistic skill. It's all about the Hollywood system having co-opted independent film festivals. I got my film awards from smaller festivals where people actually watched my film and loved it. Then it's about how no one cares if my film is great or not because I don't have a major star. So why pay a PR agent $5,000 a month just to get a Rotten Tomatoes score lower than 70 percent from white male critics?

Industry people go on and on about no one seeing indie films. Martin Scorsese wrote a Huffington op-ed about when he started out as an indie filmmaker, he'd been supported by individual reviewers, not one pathetic score by reviewers, who, by the way, are now owned by Fandango, of which Warner Brothers owns 30 percent and Comcast Universal owns 70 percent. The incentive to promote independent women filmmakers has been zero. Only now have Universal Pictures and MGM stepped forward to back a "4 percent challenge" for female directors.

The Hollywood lifestyle I've had to forego still sounds pretty fabulous, and yet I might not have ended up being writer, director, producer, and actress of films that I don't have to change because a Hollywood executive thinks his vision is better than mine. I am all for collaboration and teamwork, but when I have a vision, I don't want it compromised by a man who is a film executive and not an artist. As much as I have wanted the gilded Hollywood lifestyle and making it big with my art in my 20's, 30's, 40's and now 50's, I know 100 percent that I wouldn't have my daily meditation and yoga if the appearance of Hollywood failure hadn't forced me to value myself for my true divine self.

Maybe Leo, Jack, Marty, Jennifer, Meryl, and Charlize have found their true selves and are truly happy from the inside out. I hope so, because I want that for every human being. All I can reflect on is the life I have had and what I have learned from a (perceived) failed career. Maybe when I say goodbye to my body, I'll understand that I actually had a stellar career because I found the elixir of happiness. Everything may change around me, but my true divine nature never changes. If I feel it change, I just have to find it again because it never left me.

After 35 years, I'm finally getting awards for a film. I remain cautious, standing guard over my lower ego to keep it from cravings, obsessing on how this award isn't as good as the last one, etc. Reining myself in is essential, given how the lower ego can get caught up in endless head trips and desires.

But back to the toast Jennifer gave on that New Year's Eve, wishing *Friends* on NBC another year while never thinking it would go on for ten seasons and she would make a million dollars per episode and never have to think about money again. I wished at that moment on the dance floor, as her small hips swiveled next to mine, that I had her life and could give her toast for the New Year as my own. Now, I don't want her life and don't envy anybody's life. In my head as I write this, I hear, "You've come a long way, baby." It may be the 1968 ad selling Virginia Slims cigarettes to liberated women, but trust me, I've made it my own.

The Oxford Dictionary definition of *spiritual* is "relating to or affecting the human spirit or soul as opposed to material or physical things." That's me, baby. Everything I see, choose to see, turn on the TV to see, or talk about seeing has a spiritual component.

So what happens when you watch the violent programming so endemic to both TV and film today? You enter the consciousness state of violence and throw your soul state into hell where you participate unconsciously in the frequency of violence. This is what David Lynch's *Twin Peaks* is all about. In the intertwined Bardos we all are making our way through, we are two-way TV channels of consciousness, choosing at every moment where to dial our channel and what channel we want to dial into next.

Why did I think Jennifer had it all and that she didn't need to look for inner peace in her gilded Hollywood life? In our crazy world Bardo, we all are on the lookout for inner peace. The quest for an inner life is now a primary part of being a human being in a world in which not only is nothing permanent but in which the mind can wreak havoc on our true nature and why we are here, if we don't take good care of it. There is no avoiding taking inner peace into consideration.

So that New Year's Eve in Aspen Jennifer Aniston looked really happy, but then again she is an actress in a crowd, so even if she is dancing away and hoping to meet her dream come true, she can fake it with a smile when she has to go home alone on New Year's Eve. Eventually, of course, she did meet the most gorgeous movie star for five great years before being dumped, or maybe she said goodbye.

Good for her, you might be saying, why should I care?

Today I don't, but that night I was comparing my happiness with Jennifer Aniston's because Jennifer's happiness was about having a hit show. When I was 26 (her exact age that night), NBC and Fox were having a bidding war over who would star in the dream show I had created called *Video Dreamers*. My new agent Ari Emmanuel had dated my best friend in high school and today is one of the most powerful men in Hollywood but won't take my call. I was not only his first client but also his first client to say goodbye when the pilot was dumped. Anyway, Ari got a bidding war going between the two networks in 1988. My best friend Kristen and I had written the pilot about a young woman reporter looking for love in America and shot it with a VHS camera. When both networks made an offer, we went with the biggest and most successful, which was NBC. Hindsight being wiser than foresight, we should have gone with the riskier Fox, because they understood the *cinéma vérité* documentary-style feeling I wanted for the show, but that no one had yet done on TV.

While Fox was courting us for the show, the CEO of 20th Century Fox TV made a pass at me after dinner at a club one night, right in front of Kristen. He was married, and I was married, and I said no. NBC held onto the show for six months to "develop" it, then dropped it. We went back to Fox to face the bruised egos over our having gone with NBC first but more importantly, for not having sex with the CEO. Ari dropped me and I was dead in the water in Hollywood at 26, and here was Jennifer Aniston dancing next to me with a hit show.

Granted, I was on the local San Francisco Fox morning show as comedic entertainment reporter and could create whatever segments I wanted as long as they were no longer than two minutes, but it was still the same women-and-TV theme: the GM wanted to sleep with me and because I wouldn't, he limited me to two minutes and $150 per week. He couldn't fire me because I was too good (or because my father then wouldn't get him into a prestigious San Francisco golf club that only allowed highly recommended new members).

Now and then, I wondered if Jennifer had slept with the right person to get to the top of her game. I don't know her, but I choose to think she didn't. She is a class act all the way. I never asked her, and we all know the TV scene can be a dirty business.

The closest I ever got to speaking with her was New Year's Day when she and I were shopping in the same store.

"I was dancing right next to you last night," I said lightly, "fun party, right?"

Very nicely, like a newly famous person who is surprised anyone is bothering her while she's looking at ski jackets, she responded, "Yes, it was a lot of fun."

I looked Jennifer up on Wikipedia: "Depressed over her four unsuccessful television shows, Aniston approached Warren Littlefield at a Los Angeles gas station asking for reassurance about her career." Warren Littlefield was then running NBC TV. She was cast in Friends and the rest is history. I figured she had probably been depressed about not having a hit show the year before that New Year's Eve in

Aspen, just as I had been depressed about not having a hit show every birthday until I found meditation and yoga.

Like me, Jennifer was looking for love, and yet we both ended up depressed and divorced. Even though I didn't marry a movie star and end up on the covers of fan zines, I too went through the pain that everyone feels when they lose their best friend who turned out to be an asshole. I have no idea if Brad was truly an asshole—given that fan zines look for dirt, and if they can't find enough, create it—but now that the rumor mill is churning once again that Jennifer and Brad are picking up the strands of their old friendship, I'm guessing that, just like me, she hasn't closed her heart to love.

I look up *Friends* facts and discover that Jennifer's net worth is $200,000,000. Right now, I'm overdrawn $2,000 in each of two accounts, $4,380 to be exact, and in debt to the IRS $250,000, plus $100,000 to my good friend Lilli Rey who saved the day when I couldn't finish my film. My heat is about to be turned off, and as I write this AT&T has turned off my phone, but I can still text, and DISH TV will keep the cable on but keep me from buying any on-demand movies. Distributing a film is not cheap.

I love making people laugh, and there is no one who does it better than Jennifer. My comedic guides, gurus, and role models began with Lucille Ball and Mary Tyler Moore and continued with Julia Louis-Dreyfus, Kristen Wiig, Melissa McCarthy, and Jennifer Aniston. Gratitude for your struggles in the Hollywood Bardo, comedic heroes one and all!

Such thoughts quiet my mind about why my TV trajectory didn't work out and Jennifer's did—not that I should be comparing my life with hers if I am spiritually evolved, right?

Six years after dancing next to Jennifer Aniston, my 8-year-old daughter is obsessed with Friends. She and her best friend decided to call every listed Jennifer Aniston phone number, and they finally got her house. Her house manager said she wasn't there but would be coming from the set any minute, so could she call back? When he asked who was calling, they hung up and ran into the living room to tell me the whole story. Too cute.

# 3

# The Waitress and Mick Jagger

I approach the man and woman, both about 35, at their white Formica table. They're partners, maybe married, definitely educated.

Pencil in hand, I ask, "What will you have for breakfast?"

"What's good?" he asks.

"Pancakes, scramble with tomatoes, French toast—it's all great. This is the hottest breakfast place in San Francisco. That's why you waited an hour in line. Otherwise, why stand in line?"

They look a little shocked. What I really wanted to say was, Is one hour of your time worth pancakes, given that time is all we have here in this Bardo? Come on! I'd wait for a Rolling Stones concert, but pancakes?

They scrutinize the menu.

"Are the sausages from a local farm?"

"Yes."

"Do you know what farm?"

"No. I agree that it's important to not eat toxic meat, but I don't know the carbon footprint of this specific pig. I can ask the owner if that will make it easier for you to decide?"

If we were in Portland, I'd know, but in San Francisco I don't feel obligated to know. I've lived here for 20 years and visited since I was eight, so technically I've been coming to this beautiful city for 48 years. I was born in Chicago and everyone there is carnivorous and doesn't give a fuck where sausage is from, but San Franciscans need to know that the animals they're eating died happy and healthy; happy pigs taste better to a clear conscience.

But I'm a late night host posing as a waitress out of duress, so what do I know? Eggs are flipping and hot oil is splattering behind me.

The girlfriend gives her boyfriend the Don't ask look. "No, that's OK, we'll have the sausage and pancakes."

"To share?"

"Yes."

As I turn to put the order in, from another table I hear but pretend not to hear, "Miss . . . ?"

How did I get here? Does anyone here know where and who I was four years ago? I need a mental break. That's one of the advantages of jobs like waitressing: for the most part, you still have your own headspace.

*I flash back to when my ex-husband was once my adored fiancé who was like family. (That he was like family should have been a clue as to how things would turn out.) I desperately wanted a family that would work. While we were having a drink in a West Village bar one month after our engagement announcement, I told him I wouldn't be changing my last name when we were married. He was not happy about that, though it was 1988 and women were just beginning to keep their birth surnames. I tried to cheer him up by telling him that I would never have a marital affair unless—*

*He interrupted. "Isn't not having a marital affair a given? It's one of the Ten Commandments."*

*"But—"*

*"There is no but."*

*I continued. "We're engaged and I love you, but if I meet Mick Jagger, I will sleep with him."*

*He was speechless.*

*"Technically," I assuaged, "it wouldn't be an affair since Mick's a rock star and sleeps with one woman after*

*another. And would I feel guilty about his wife Jerry Hall who signed up to be married to a rock star? No."*

*"You're serious," aka Dickhead six years later said as it dawned on him that I was serious. "What about me?"*

*It all seemed logical to me. "That's why I'm telling you now. You have a right to know my one condition of marrying."*

*He countered, "OK, if I meet Daryl Hannah, I will sleep with her."*

*Back then, Daryl Hannah was a drop-dead beautiful movie star from Splash dating John F. Kennedy, Jr. My fiancé was equally drop-dead gorgeous.*

*"Not a problem. Perfect, we've got a deal."*

*As Fate would have it, once we were married, we lived in my husband's glorious Village loft apartment on the same floor as Keith Richards, with Cher coming by to ask for a cup of sugar (uh huh). I saw Keith with Patti Hansen one Saturday night. Patti asked us to hold the elevator while she yelled down the hallway, "Keith, the elevator is here, hurry up!" In the elevator, Keith stared at the floor, the only real option for private thoughts in elevators. You've got to admire a man still rocking at 75 years old.*

*Keith seemed to me to be how he's presented in his autobiography: humble, kind, talented, and for the most part joyful, despite having been a drug addict for years. Most who've ingested half the drugs and alcohol Keith has ingested are dead in one way or another. I figured that, like Rumpelstiltskin, he must know how to alchemize substances into gold (including his rumored youthful blood transfusions). Drugs and rock stars go together, but isn't it partially due to having to endure endless staring people and nosy neighbors like me? My husband called me from his Wall Street day trading job one morning to say I'd missed Keith and guitarist Ronnie Wood leaving their loft apartment at 7 am after an all-nighter. I immediately regretted not having been there in my husband's pajamas to pass something, anything, to him that he'd forgotten.*

*I wasn't sure who I loved more, Keith or Mick. The Rolling Stones inspired me like no other band, helping me through my darkest times. Their music elevated me. The only other band equal to the Stones for me is Pearl Jam. The Who and Led Zeppelin were my high school bands, but the Stones and Pearl Jam got me through the ups and downs of adult life.*

*The honeymoon phase of my one marriage began in that illustrious Village loft with joy, happiness, and undying passionate love, then devolved into the old familiar themes of verbal abuse, manipulation and control that made me feel powerless. I could escape physically but not emotionally—just as with my father. By the time I left six years later and had my 18-month-old daughter only 50 percent of the time, I felt the same loneliness and powerlessness I had felt in the two homes I'd grown up in, neither of which was ever really my home. I had unconsciously repeated what I knew, what I had grown up with.*

*Is that what "falling in love" is really about? An opportunity to make conscious another piece of the Bardo, namely one's family of origin patterns?*

*Be here now was the Buddhist mandate of the Sixties. Did it help when it came to getting through the Hollywood Bardo? I'd thought about meeting Mick Jagger since I was 16 years old and finally met him when I was 34—a dream that took 18 years to materialize. Now, I indulged myself by revisiting the memory over and over, far from* Be here now.

Back on planet Earth, I eye the sixteen tables lined up in an L and head for table 8.

"Hi, what would you like today?"

"We waited an hour and fifteen minutes in line, and now another 15 minutes."

"I'm so sorry, sir, but we are so busy. What can I get you?"

"Maybe a job well done?"

I consider taking a bat to his head and screaming, Do you know what I used to do? But I don't, because I'd be fired, and I am a single mother with a 7-year-old and can't afford to be homeless, even if my father owns a huge hotel chain and will likely never let me live in his home.

"What would you like to eat this morning?"

"An omelette . . ."

I write the order up, not caring what this man eats, just as he doesn't care that my late night host dream is over and will never be realized. What would Be here now Ram Dass say about my mind craving refuge in the best memory of my life? Does being mentally somewhere and sometime else come under "multitasking"?

I get the next table's order, pick up omelettes, coffee, orange juice, low-fat milk. Each morning I fill the little pitchers of half-and-half when I arrive at 7:45 after dropping my daughter at the school bus. All the while, deep in my mind, I am to one degree or another savoring Mick Jagger, my go-to memory when things are dark and I'm trying not to give up on my dream.

*In my tight red leather outfit and 3-inch black thin-strap heels, I'm in the Ritz Carlton elevator. I've just given the secret password Mick had whispered into my ear at the Fillmore to the front desk clerk.*

*"'Grace' is on the 8th floor," she says as she picks up the phone.*

*Once I'm in the elevator, a huge linebacker security guard, his hand between the doors to keep them from closing, steps in and pushes 6 instead of 8, saying, "You can't go to floor 8 right now."*

*We wait, the ten floor numbers beaming back at me from their little white circles. I remember this elevator from a charity event I attended. What floor was it on?*

*I sink into a child's sadness when her favorite toy is taken away and she has to take a nap. I can't just push 8 and* go to "Grace," so I wait, knowing I can't ask why I can't go right to floor 8.

Finally, he says into his walkie-talkie, "She's here," and the radio responds, "Have her wait . . ."

The rock god Mick, flanked by two security guards, passes the open elevator door and gives me a look from deep-blue intelligent eyes that says, Say anything and you won't be coming up. I am dead silent as I watch him pass. The last guard in his retinue says to my security guard, "Sixth floor." The elevator door closes. At the 6th floor, I'm told to follow him. At a corner in the hallway, he says, "We have to wait here."

Twelve minutes pass as I wait in dead silence, patiently staring at a Ritz Carlton wall, thinking and praying that I will be led back into the elevator and head for the 8th floor. I spend the time going over how all of this came to pass.

The Bridges to Babylon Tour ran from 1997 to 1998. Who would have imagined that the Stones would tour for so many years nonstop—50 years, to be exact? They'd taken a break in the 80's, maybe due to differences between Mick and Keith. I was 34 years old, divorced, and recently on TV as a comedy/entertainment reporter. Mick's friend Johnny Pigozzi, whom I had met at the Le Lipp Brasserie in Paris, had shown Mick my tape of me chasing him in a short skirt and high heels outside the Ritz Carlton during the Voodoo Lounge Tour in 1994. Mick was now in San Francisco and Johnny had said he would have Mick call me. I waited and waited, going to each of the Babylon shows with Pearl Jam opening at the Oakland Coliseum, but the phone never rang. I then figured out a way to get invited to the private party at the Fillmore where the Stones were to perform. My plan was to leave with him, so my friends had driven me and left because they didn't want to wait more than two hours since it was midnight on a Sunday night, when the band finally arrived in rock'n'roll style. Even my brother said, "I'm out of here, even if it is Mick." So I sat alone waiting for Mick with an open bar, needing cash only for a *taxi. After 17 years of thinking about one goal, I was determined to end up at Mick's hotel.*

*Sure enough, the Stones walked in at midnight and went immediately upstairs to the private room so it would be impossible for anyone uninvited to get into. I dropped the name Johnny Pigozzi to the Stones' manager, adding that I was supposed to meet Mick here (a white lie), and the golden door opened. There was Mick surrounded by people. Because I am almost six feet tall in high heels, he saw me right away and came over to speak to me.*

*"Marcia, your tape made me laugh. I loved it. Are you sticking around? I have a few people I need to talk to . . ."*

*"Of course," I said, thinking, I am going home with you. I have thought about this for 17 years.*

*I sat waiting patiently for an eternity for Mick to ask me to join him at his friends' table. Johnny Depp walked up to say hello to Mick and sat right next to me. Mick on my left, Johnny on my right—two of my favorite all-time artists, and it wasn't a dream. I remember thinking that if my rock god didn't ask me, I could always go home with Johnny—not that he asked, but maybe the thought crossed his mind, and he was single at the time.*

*So goes the Hollywood Bardo.*

*At 2 am, the lights flashed on and off and Mick whispered, "Do you want to come back to the hotel?"*

*I smiled Yes, at which Mick said, "Leave after me because there may be photographers out front. At the desk, use the code name 'Grace.'"*

*It was unlikely that photographers would be outside, because San Francisco is such a sleepy town, but this was, after all, the king of rock'n'roll.*

*Mick stood up and said his goodbyes.*

*I grabbed him and whispered, "You forgot to tell me the hotel."*

*He laughed. "The Ritz Carlton." I think he assumed I knew because of the comedy segment I had done two years before...*

The waitress that is me stares at the big ticking clock in the restaurant, urging it to say 3 pm so I can leave. How can it only be 9:30 am and breakfast still in full tilt?

"Scrambled eggs with mushrooms and onions and a side of bacon?" I am barely listening to myself.

"Yes, but I think my son wants a side of pancakes. Do you have those small silver dollar stacks?"

"No."

The bratty kid says, "Then I don't want them."

The father who can't discipline his child says to his bratty son, "They taste the same, they're just bigger."

"I don't want them unless they're small, they don't taste the same."

He slams his fist on the table. I refrain from saying, "Who the fuck cares if pancakes are small or big? You are wrong, kid. People are starving in Mali, be grateful you have food."

But I don't say that because I need to pay for my daughter's Halloween costume and school supplies, and if we're lucky, a new used car. Thank God my thoughts are my own, including my refuge in Mick.

"We don't have silver dollar pancakes."

"But I want pancakes," the kid whines.

"Sir, I can see if the cook will make them smaller, but usually they don't do special orders because, as you can see, we are so busy."

"Ah, thank you." He turns to his son. "What do you say?"

The brat says nothing.

"Will you please say thank you to the waitress."

Nothing from the kid.

"I'll put the order in."

"I'm so sorry he didn't say thank you. He should, but I can't make him."

"No big deal."

Which was not true. It is a big deal. I can't advise parents, "Raise your kid right and you won't have a nightmare later." If this father could hear it from a late night host he randomly met in a restaurant or on my late night show, he might listen, but I am a waitress and therefore lack the status to comment on parenting. I put the order in as my mind races back to the night that would surely get me through the rest of this day.

*From the walkie-talkie comes, "Bring her up, he's ready now." The security guard and I walk to the elevator. He pushes 8. I am on my way up to heaven.*

*Trembling, I walk down the 8th floor hallway. At the door, I ask the security guard, "What should I do?"*

*"Knock."*

*How many women have entered his rooms in different cities around the world? Am I the only one entering tonight? Maybe, maybe not.*

*The door opens and there he is in his purple shirt, striped maroon pants, and thin black shoes. He grabs my hand and thanks the security guard. The door closes and immediately he starts kissing me like I'm a long-awaited dinner. I stop him. After all, he is 20 years older than me and I'd never been with an older man. He is 54 and a stranger and I don't kiss strangers that quickly, even if that stranger is Mick Jagger . . .*

The kid is screaming, "I don't like the pancakes. Too big!"

"They're fine. Thank you, miss, for trying to make this work."

The child shoves the plate onto the floor and it shatters.

Slowly, I stoop to pick up shards of porcelain with my left hand and sticky pancake residue with my right hand, pondering what evil I did in my last life to merit being a waitress and not the Queen of Late Night as I'd dreamed, or at the very least Johnny Depp's girlfriend.

I toss the brat's breakfast in a bin in the restaurant closet and grab a broom, my mind clutching at Mick.

*Coquettishly, I pull away from him. "I'm so happy to be here, but how about a glass of wine? I'm really nervous."*

*He smiles.*

*I follow him through the living room and past a bedroom to the small kitchen. The master bedroom down the hall has a king-sized bed with a purple duvet. I catch a glimpse of at least 60 outfits hanging in a portable closet rack. The suite is bigger than my 1500-square-foot apartment in North Beach. I am sweating head to toe but seem to be keeping my cool. No doubt Mick has been down this road so many times that quelling panic attacks of excitement and fear in young women is a norm.*

*A bottle of red wine is on the counter but not an opener. The king of rock'n'roll opens every drawer in the kitchen but no opener. He heads back to the living room and opens every drawer.*

*"Is it all right if I look at your stage clothes rack?" I ask.*

*"Sure," he says, still opening and closing drawers.*

*I feel like I am voyeuring someone's sex toys. I go from one sparkly jacket to another—a silver glittery one, a gold sparkly one, purple velvet, rainbow . . . I want to pull each jacket out, wear it, savor its beauty and style, walk around in it—but I don't. I need to stop and contain my excitement, keep things cool. Otherwise, I am gone, moving quickly from heaven to hell. Like when he stared into my elevator, each minute is about passing or not passing a test. So I leave the clothing rack that I so desperately want to examine and go back into the living room where he is still looking for a wine opener. I get a glimmer of the man who had lived six lifetimes of sex, drugs, and rock'n'roll, who had brought so much great music to millions of fans. Larger than life on stage, in real life he has a small frame and is of average height but not average everywhere. I watch him walk and it is as if he glides or floats, his shoes barely touching the carpet.*

*He doesn't call room service for a wine opener but at last after 15 minutes finds one. Proud of himself, he glides to the kitchen and soon has a glass of Bordeaux for me.*

*I sip and inanely ask, "How do you shop for all those jackets?"*

*"I set up appointments after hours when stores are closed."*

*"Do you pick all your clothing for the tour?"*

*"Most of it."*

*We sit on the couch. The wine is helping me relax and I finally accept that I am sitting with Mick Jagger as I had imagined so many times. It isn't a dream.*

*"Why isn't there a female lead singer who has even come close to you? I can only think of Madonna and Tina Turner, but they aren't you." This was long before Lady Gaga or Beyoncé, but they're not Mick, either.*

*"I don't know," he smiles.*

*He isn't drinking with me. He doesn't drink much on tour. I wonder what he was like in the 70's when I was a teenager, women throwing themselves at him, married to Bianca . . . He leans over and kisses me—the best kisser ever— then grabs me and puts me on his lap, breaking into mad passionate kissing like I'm the only woman in his life . . .*

*When I leave hours later, he asks if I'll be at the show tomorrow and I quip, "Me and 35,000 fans."*

*He laughs. "I'll get you a backstage pass. Come and say hello."*

*The next night I have a blind date who is proud of having gotten 4ᵗʰ row center seats. I can't tell anyone but my closest friends about my backstage pass. My date picks me up late, and it is pouring when we arrive just as the Stones are about to start. I race backstage and am stopped by a security guard. I show him my pass.*

*"The party's over, the Stones are about to start," the guard says.*

*"Mick Jagger told me to drop by and say hello," I respond.*

*The security guard smirks. "Right, lady."*

*All of a sudden, the entire band exits the elevator and starts walking to the stage, but the guard has pushed me so far from the stage that I can't say hello. As the band waits for the curtains to open, something makes Mick turn around. We're about 25 years from each other. He smiles, walks down the stage stairs, and heads for me. Reaching me, he gives me a kiss on the cheek and says, "Marcia, it's no nice you made it, but unfortunately we have a show to put on."*

*The security guard is dumbfounded as Mick returns to the band. "Go wherever you want," he says to me.*

*"Ladies and gentlemen, it's the Rolling Stones!"*

*I sneak behind the long stage where Mick is running back and forth. He sees me and turns his back on 35,000 screaming fans, sings the song to me, then races off.*

*I return to my 4$^{th}$ row center seat.*

*Two days later, my phone rings.*

*"I would like to thank you for the corkscrew."*

*It didn't occur to me that what I called a wine opener was also a corkscrew. "Who is this?" I asked.*

*"Mick Jagger," the voice said.*

*"Is this a joke?" I asked.*

*"No, it's really Mick."*

*"Mick, is that you?"*

*"Yes, Marcia. It was so sweet of you to drop off a tiffany corkscrew."*

*Ah, the wine opener! "Well, Mick, for a brief moment, the man who had everything lacked a wine opener. Now, you'll never be without."*

The waitress that is me is at last off-duty and on her way home to her daughter. I take a final look at the waitresses coming on shift, checking their condiments, adjusting their aprons. Finally at 38 years old, I feel the fact that millions of people do service jobs all their lives. Everyone should wait tables for a while so they have the opportunity to learn to treat all stations of life better, Mick Jagger or no Mick Jagger.

# 4

# Women in Late Night

Did childhood unhappiness and escape into TV-land lead me to comedy? To an extent, yes, but there was more that I seemed to have brought with me into this life.

In third grade, when I was eight or nine years old, I was already a natural producer. I worked on floats for the local parade and wrote and produced plays with my stepsister, who 45 years later would be awarded a Pulitzer Prize for her mind-bending novel. I longed to perform in these plays. At school I auditioned but couldn't remember my lines. (I was an ad-lib girl from the beginning.) I recall rejection after rejection—for example, as president of my class—but kept going and eventually won.

At home, I loved watching *I Love Lucy* reruns (1951-1957),[3] Rowan and Martin's *Laugh-In* (1968-1973), *The Mary Tyler Moore Show* (1970-1977), *The Carol Burnett Show* (1967-1978), *Sonny and Cher Comedy Hour* (1971-1974) . . . Comedy wasn't just about escape; it was about how natural it felt to be choosing entertainment as my future profession and path. In my conscious mind, I've always been convinced that I had the talent and that if I worked hard to get a break, all would turn out well. What I didn't know was the omnipresence

---

[3] Lucille and her Cuban bandleader husband Desi Arnaz (Desilu Productions) were embroiled in Cold War politics. Not only was CBS reluctant to show a pregnant ("expecting") woman on air, but they also didn't like her having a Cuban husband. Diversity was scarce in Cold War America.

of the hidden labyrinthine Hollywood Bardo that weaves in and out of talent and breaks.

Goldie Hawn on *Laugh-in* (1967-1973) was a great comedic/dramatic actress (*Private Benjamin,* 1980; etc.) and one of the first groundbreaking woman producers, along with Jane Fonda (*Coming Home*, 1978; etc.).[4] What did those powerful women go through in order to produce such amazing movies while remaining artists of integrity? Both hugely influenced me, along with Lucy and Mary, while *Wonder Woman* (1975-1979) made me wonder, Can any woman truly become a Wonder Woman? More to the point, can a woman be Wonder Woman and not have to show off a sexualized body?

For my 28th birthday, I asked my father for a $5,000 Beta tape deck for editing so I could make my own comedy segments. I had never asked for more than a $1,000 gift, but he was a millionaire by then, having started the Kimpton Hotels a decade earlier. This one birthday gift literally changed my life. It was so empowering to be able to create, master, and change media content, despite my father not supporting my dreams of comedy, acting, and producing my own show. Even with the experience of such a tool, it took me eight years to get on TV. I was so close so many times, but it never happened. The formula of talent, hard work, and a break were foolproof, right? But from 22 on, I was herded toward settling for being a secretary or production assistant (PA).

*Rock'n'Roll Evening News*

My first *Aha*! regarding the massive challenge awaiting any woman setting her sights on making it in the Hollywood Bardo began at Indiana University when I was going with Jim

---

[4] Goldie lives right around the block from me on a gorgeous ranch. Her nonprofit MindUP *https://mindup.org/coming-soon.html* is where my first big check is going because it's about teaching meditation to kids to strengthen their minds and prevent mental illness. I wrote the check already, but it can't be cashed with $500,000 film debt.

(see chapter 6). He was the real-deal campus activist who introduced me to the Student Union board where I became the lectures director and discovered that I was really a producer whose greatest joy was birthing creative ideas into reality. My budget was $20,000, a lot of money for a 20 year old to be in charge of.

Former directors had organized four lectures to my 88, which included bringing CBS *Sunday Morning* anchor Jane Pauley to speak at her alma mater. In 1982, when only Johnny Carson was hosting on TV, Jane was my dream host whose morning slot was bigger and more popular than Johnny's late night. My goal was either to head to Hollywood for a rock'n'roll show or to NYC to become Jane Pauly's replacement when she decided to retire.

After Jane spoke, she, Jim, and I ended up at the IU's hottest bar, Nick's, having a beer. Jane said she rarely drank in college because she'd been working so hard to succeed. The idea of doing without alcohol and pot went right over my head, though obviously it had paid off for Jane, who was on national TV by the time she was 25. She was so intelligent, classy, and beautiful! When I walked her to her hotel room, she said emphatically, "Marcia, you should be a producer. That is exactly what you did tonight: you produced a perfect evening." Back then, I didn't even know what a producer was; I could only imagine being a host. But I had been producing events since I was seven. Jane invited me to NYC to see the *Today* show live and meet the producers.

Two months later over spring break, I flew to NYC and met everyone at the top of NBC. A dream come true, I thought, I'm set for my career and life. But unlike Jane, it would take me until I was 32, not 25, to be live, not on national TV, but on KTVU-SF. I asked *Today* for an internship, but they had no internships then. Instead, they set me up with the NBC affiliate in Phoenix that summer, where I stared at a wall when I wasn't in the editing room learning about editing. I called Jane to say I wasn't learning anything and if I was going to stare at the wall, why couldn't I stare at the NYC Today show wall? She agreed, and I returned to NYC.

It was magical to observe how the live *Today* show worked! I got to sit in the TV control booth with Steve Friedman screaming into Bryant Gumbel's or Jane's ear while they remained calm and cool.

At NBC, there was one female executive, and Jane made a serious point of introducing me to her. Nancy headed up NBC promotions and was as bright and beautiful as Jane. Later, after I graduated, the Today show offered me $13,000 ($39,000 in 2018 dollars) as a PA and Nancy couldn't really help me. I wonder how different my life would have been if I had accepted, but I couldn't imagine living on that little in Queens, plus there was the 1980's crime fest, nor could I imagine not creating my dream rock'n'roll late night show.

Only after years of meditation and spiritual studies did I realize that I had the power to change my TV channel from moment to moment. This is exactly how we choose or create our lives. If you believe it's just the luck of the draw and the only life you'll ever get, you may one day make the terrible decision to not survive, despite fighting as hard as you can, like my brother did. I cannot judge his choice; under certain circumstances, some people just can't change the channel. I suffered years of depression and felt powerless over it, but that very suffering led to awakening to who I truly am and how I can keep consciously creating the life I choose instead of the life unconsciously chosen for me by my ancestors, family, society, etc.

After graduation, I spent two years working as a PA on every rock video of the early MTV days, running out at 4 am to pick up free donuts and make sure the cast and crew had fresh coffee. In order to survive the mental hell of just serving coffee and donuts, I wrote *Rock'n'Roll Evening News*, my first production. But the producer I brought the TV script/pilot to registered it at the Writers Guild of America (WGA) under his name. I didn't even know what the WGA was. When he showed me his name on the registration, I asked why my name wasn't on it and he said I was too young.

When I heard by accident about the power lunch at the Palm Restaurant at which the unnamed producer was going to pitch *Rock'n'Roll Evening News*, I ran down the hall to the head of the production company and said, "I heard [the unnamed producer] is meeting with Irving Azoff to get a record label associated with the show. I wrote that show, and Irving is the one who got me my first job in the business. I need to be there."

He shrugged, said OK, picked up the phone and called the unnamed producer.

Irving Azoff, then the president of the MCA Music Entertainment Group after tremendous success as the Eagles manager, asked, "Who wrote it? It's great."

At first, the unnamed producer was off and running with the lie that he had written it, but then guilt or getting caught made him self-correct and admit that I had, all in front of Irving, who to this day is the most powerful man in the music business.[5]

Irving passed, but was obviously impressed by what I'd created. Next, we went to Warner Brothers Records to pitch the script because we needed the backing and credibility of a record company if we were going to do a news show about music. Eight male executives[6] of Warner Brothers TV Studios were there, too, too hear our TV pitch. (Warner Brothers was where Wonder Woman and Laugh-in had been filmed and Friends would be filmed later.) Because the producer who stole my script was incapable of answering their questions because he didn't know the ideas I had written and had barely read the pilot, I ended up being the one to pitch it.

---

[5] "In 2012, he topped *Billboard*'s Power 100 and was named the most powerful person in the music industry." - Wikipedia

[6] Only two women have risen to head up major Hollywood studios: Sherry Lansing (Paramount Pictures) and Dawn Steel (Columbia Pictures), who unfortunately died of brain cancer at 49.

They passed on the pilot, too, but I'll never forget the confidence I felt knowing my creative ideas would work if I were left in charge of them.

After selling the idea to A&M Records, at the time a hot record company that had just signed Shirley Crow, we needed more financing from a bigger production company, so we went to the King Brothers, Michael and Roger, as they were launching *The Oprah Winfrey Show* from Chicago. I was the only woman there and was late because I'd been copying *Rock'n'Roll Evening News* ideas into a booklet for the pilot. As I entered and began handing out copies, Roger King quipped in front of his brother Michael King of King World, "Marcia is here now because she has big tits," a comment meant to wound and shame me. It stopped me in my tracks, but I bit my tongue, knowing that if I said anything in response, I would be fired. Misogyny, woman as body, deceit, sexploitation—these are Bardo parameters women who hope to "make it" in Hollywood must be prepared to deal with.

I'll never forget that moment, nor will I forget the loose-fitting dress that etched into my psyche forever the fact that in Hollywood, how a woman looks matters more than what she says or does. With all its dime-a-dozen starlets, Hollywood is still an alpha male jungle kingdom.

Until my 30's, I never showed off my body. When I got breasts, my stepfather tutored me over and over, "Marcia, never depend on your looks. Always depend on your mind." One day in 1978 when I was 16 and sunbathing on our lawn, he came home early and punished me for wearing a bikini. How grateful I am to him for attempting to arm me! But at 24, I still wasn't prepared for Hollywood's double standard: women valued for their appearance, men for their cunning and notches in their belt. My father had his own generational sexism. When I was 13 and eating my third bowl of cereal, he reminded me that if I kept up like that, I'd be fat. He ended up driving his wife, stepdaughter, and a few girlfriends to anorexia, but I chose instead to struggle going up and down ten pounds my entire life. To be fair, when my father's hotel business started, he gave Juliana Bancroft a high position (and named his third hotel after her!), then later gave Equinox CEO Niki Leondakis a huge opportunity.

Despite the crass remark, I still thought that *Rock'n'Roll Evening News* would report on music and culture from around the world while discovering new talent, and I would have the opportunity I'd dreamed of since watching Dick Clark on American Bandstand when I was 12. I would have my own late night show like Lucy and Mary, make people laugh with my original ideas, and of course make millions of dollars.

But when I asked the unnamed producer if I could be on camera, he said no, because I dressed like a Midwesterner and didn't highlight my hair like Eleanor Mondale. The daughter of former Vice President Walter Mondale under Jimmy Carter (1977-1981) was at that time on the local LA station, was from the Midwest, and looked exactly like me except for her highlights and better clothes.[7] My stolen renamed show (unnamed so the unnamed producer doesn't sue me) was finally picked up by King World Productions, which was also producing *The Oprah Winfrey Show*, *Wheel of Fortune*, and *Jeopardy*.

When the photo of the opening party for the show made it into the Hollywood Reporter, the unnamed producer was credited with the show, and I was named production assistant. I felt so abandoned. He not only stole my idea but removed me from the huge office with great views from downtown to the beach (that now holds the Soho House), hired a staff of 15, and shoved me, the PA, into a closet he'd pulled file cabinets and junk out of—all to hide his crime. I stayed because I had to pay the rent, but once I figured out a way to save money I left for New York City and worked on Wall Street to make money for

---

[7] Eleanor got the job at CBS I wanted but died of a brain tumor by 50. Would that have been me?

my TV ideas. After 16 months, I left for Jim, whom I had dated through college and now lived in London. When the head of Bear Stearns said, "So you're leaving for your vagina?" he was right, but it was also about not being able to get passionate about selling money (even if it was nice to make it) and the sexist weirdness of being asked to cut my bra when we got a trade. There was only one female partner in the firm in 1986. Quite a few people had left to work for Sandler O'Neill & Partners and died in the World Trade Center on 9/11.

When I finally got on TV in San Francisco, I tracked that unnamed producer down so I could complete a full emotional circle. He was working for King World Productions, and his only comment when he saw me again with my highlighted blond hair and black leather pants was, "You look great, Marcia." He had no idea of how he had devastated me at 24. Up until then, I had been a good girl from the Midwest who couldn't believe that people could lie, cheat, and steal just to get ahead. He introduced me to the reality of Hollywood peppered with a few good people like Ron Howard.

*Video Dreamers*

In 1987, Fox and NBC fought a bidding war over my dream late night show *Video Dreamers*—the tale of a young woman reporter traveling across America in search of love— that I had created with Kristen, my best friend since college. One of the biggest agents in Hollywood who had just joined the Creative Artists Agency (CAA) pitched our show to Fox and NBC.

There had never been a show done in the *cinéma vérité* documentary style mixing a fictional and nonfictional script—a scripted show with fictional characters on the streets of America asking Americans real questions. Kristen held the VHS camera and I acted with another lead actor, then we edited it for the pilot. I loved editing: For me, the story is credited in the editing room and not on the page. This was the third production I had done with a creative team of only two people, with Kristen as my collaborator.

During the bidding war, I took the train from NYC downtown to Hoboken across the river to find a psychic recommended to me as the best psychic ever. She was only 26, which was how old I was at the time, and worked in her dark basement. Four years earlier in LA, my first psychic said that I would be the next Barbara Stanwyck, the legendary actress who had been the wealthiest and most successful woman in the U.S. I'll never forget what this second psychic said to me. It's as if it happened yesterday.

She asked me to pick three cards from her deck. I don't remember what I picked, but after looking at them, she said, "You are going to become very famous and successful in everything you've dreamed, but it will be when you are much older."

So it wasn't going to happen after the bidding war between NBC and Fox. At 26, this was bad news.

"How old?"

"Really old."

"I don't understand." Everyone said she was the best psychic ever, so she was a success at 26, right?

"That's what I hear for you, and I know it will happen."

I stare at her. "How old again?"

"Old," she says sagely, "50-plus."

To an extent, the word old is relative. At 26 you think 38 is old, at 36 you think 48 is old, and at 46 you think 58 is really, really fucking old. I am 56 writing this and 57 finishing the book, so when the fuck is fame going to happen? Hollywood cranks out cash daily, so why not crank it out for women directors and queens of late night?

Listening to her in 1987, I'm thinking, *How do you really know?* If psychics were 100 percent right, they would be millionaires because they would know exactly what to do and when in the stock market. They wouldn't hang out little signs like "Walk right in, palm readings $5." But this psychic's reputation preceded her, and I now realize it's all in the interpretation—for example, the success of achieving the dream of *Bardo Blues*. As for the Oscar . . .

Her last "old" overwhelmed me with sadness. I didn't want to wait years. Twenty-one-year-old Julia Roberts had just hit it big with *Mystic Pizza* and in 1990 would hit it even bigger with *Pretty Woman*. That was supposed to be me! Years later, thanks to his daughter Lori, I met *Pretty Woman* and *Happy Days* director Garry Marshall and thanked him for all the joy he had provided me. In 1996, he was awarded the Women in Film Crystal + Lucy Award in recognition of excellence and innovation in creative works enhancing the perception of women through the medium of television. He was someone I had always dreamed of working with, but it never happened.

At 26, I couldn't foresee the lessons probably already waiting for me: rejection after rejection in the entertainment business to a total of 35 years, a horrible divorce and brutal custody battle, my daughter taken from me by the court system, her Thai parasite undiagnosed for years, my late night show going off the air in 14 weeks, the lawsuit my *Live From the Starlight Room* director subjected me to, my father on his deathbed refusing to talk to me, my brother's suicide . . .

It may all have been to ultimately help me heal my wounded inner child, but at 26, my career was in the forefront of my mind. I had done all the acting and reporting classes at respectable studios like Lee Strasberg that I could. I didn't want to study anymore. I wanted my own TV series and knew I was talented enough to become a star. Not to mention that Hollywood doesn't embrace ageing. I wanted my dream to happen tomorrow! I didn't yet see the grander and deeper schemes of life, much less how much time they took to accomplish. Only my higher self saw it. Had I become famous at 26 as I'd dreamed, happiness and peace would still have evaded me.

In short, I didn't want the psychic's prediction.

73

But she was right. I sat there on my bed in a panic attack, waiting night after night to hear when I would be on TV. But my dream sit-com show *Video Dreamers* was dropped six months later by a female TV executive my age. We should have gone with Fox the risk-taker (e.g. The Simpsons) and not my dream network NBC. My dream was never realized, so once again I was stuck with no validation for being on TV or working hard part-time so I could be there for my daughter.

## Last Call

When I think of all the TV projects I've tried to sell (ten, to be exact) and what the gifted psychic told me, I think of guys like the Fox GM at the San Francisco KTVU station who wanted to have sex with me. Once I said no, he limited me to two minutes on the air and $150 a week for four years, even after my father got him into the prestigious golf club in San Francisco. (The Fox GM said I didn't need more money because my father was rich.)

When my pilot late night show *Last Call* was shot at the Bimbo Club in San Francisco and then aired on KTVU-Fox, our ratings beat out Saturday Night Live, and yet the following Monday, the Fox GM pulled me into his office to tell me how awful I was on camera and to give up on my dream of having my own show. It was 1996 and I was 34 years old.

But I continued hustling and scrambling for a sprinter to my Last Call late night show for over a year. Finally, San Francisco Giants CEO Larry Baer liked my TV segments and called his friend, Seattle Seahawks CEO Peter McLoughlin, who loved the Last Call tape and committed to $2,000 per show. Budweiser had never backed a local show but would do it for me if San Francisco KTVU-Fox played my late night show on Saturday evenings. After the third show ratings didn't beat out *Saturday Night Live*—in the beginning they had, and with a budget of $2,000 per show and not $2 million—they moved me to 1:30 am.

Fourteen weeks later, my dream late night show was off the air and I was $150,000 in debt to the crew.

I recall a conversation with head anchor Ross over lunch outside the TV station before I left for KGO-ABC that should have gone off like a light bulb in my head, but didn't— not yet, anyway. When I told him about all my bad breaks with GMs, he said, "I just can't understand what's going on." I naively agreed, never thinking the "bad breaks" came straight from the unwritten requirement that I sleep with the GMs. (Surely Ryan Seacrest hadn't been in that situation for the Fox *Morning Show*?)

For my last day at KTVU after four years of watching the morning show and longing to be on the air more than just one day a week, the editor and I had compiled my best segments to show as my goodbye. But the Fox GM couldn't resist getting one last punch in. He insisted he had to go on live to talk about a "local matter," thus cutting my minutes so I had no way of saying goodbye and thanking the station. My clips ran, and we were off the air in 30 seconds.

*Live From the Starlight Room*

The second I got Budweiser to sponsor my new late night show *Live From the Starlight Room,* I used my last divorce settlement dollars to produce the show since I didn't have enough from Budweiser, and moved to KGO, San Francisco ABC's affiliate station. I sold my BMW to pay for production, and thanks to my father, I got the Starlight Room, San Francisco's most historic nightclub, for free. I produced, wrote, hosted and booked all the shows with comedy segments and 18 bands for 14 shows in 8 days. It taught me I could do anything if I wanted it bad enough, even if I needed more money and more crew. Producing 14 shows in 8 days with no money in the bank and a crew cash-flowed out over the year was doing the impossible (until my next two films *My Reality* and *Bardo Blues*). Any late night host or filmmaker should be able to do this, but as a woman you have to always do the impossible or it won't get done.

Budweiser's $2,000 per week paid the crew for working so incredibly hard to put together 14 shows in 8 days, all the while taking a delayed paycheck so I could get local talent. Who produces a late night show for $2,000 per show and cash-flows the rest out to the crew? But I still didn't have enough money. The divorce money and the little bit my father was sending weren't quite enough, not to mention that my part-time job was a fulltime job.

Then the GM who liked me at KGO was fired. Like a rerun of KTVU, they brought in an asshole whose rumored profile included firing employees on Christmas Eve with only two weeks severance. I had gotten Budweiser, but we couldn't have anticipated the KGO GM being fired and an asshole GM taking me off the air, and when I tried to ask for a 3 am slot, said no and ran infomercials. As we were editing the third show on four hours of sleep per night, the new GM announced that I would be off the air in 14 weeks, knowing full well he was putting me in $150,000 debt and probably thinking my rich Kimpton Hotels dad would help me out.

I was 38 years old, broke, and my latest late night show dream had come to an end. I left my daughter with her father for a week and drove to Bakersfield, Fresno, Eureka, etc., to sell VHS copies of the shows. In the summer, while I drove to Indianapolis, Cleveland, Columbus, Denver, Durango, Phoenix, Houston, and Abilene, my daughter stayed with her grandparents just outside Chicago. I got another eight stations to put my show on once a week but none in the top markets. I remember almost begging station managers in Houston and Dallas to put my show on, but they didn't. I will never forget the GM in Bakersfield who was so impressed by me driving across America with my VHS copies to show GMs and syndicate them myself that he put me on just for that reason and no other.

I was a mini-version of the King Brothers who had gone from station to station in America basically starting the syndication business by selling *Wheel of Fortune* and *Jeopardy*, with their jackpot being *The Oprah Winfrey Show* in Chicago, which I watched while growing up. The King Brothers were also the first to syndicate The *Rock'n'Roll Evening News*, and now I was doing exactly what they had done in 1985 for *Oprah*.[8]

The King Brothers sold their company for $2.5 billion in 1999 to CBS, and all because *Oprah* created $210 million in cash flow. Oprah today is worth $2.6 billion—rightly so because no one was better on daytime TV. But I wanted a female late night, forbidden in the 80's and 90's, and it's the same today.

When I had 12 stations committed (the King Brothers got commitments from 250 stations), I showed up at the National Association of Television Program Executives (NAPTE) and tried to sell it to every GM who passed my little booth, outshone by the King brothers nearby. Then I flew to St. Louis and begged ten Budweiser executives to pay for ads in Fresno, Bakersfield, etc., but they wouldn't, because it wasn't a large market, they never do local shows, and they couldn't make an exception if I was not in one of the top five major markets. They would, however, pay for my show at 3 am in San Francisco, but I couldn't get a meeting with the asshole GM to beg him. I had commitments to the stations that basically were paying me nothing unless I had ratings, and even if I could beat out *Saturday Night Live* on my first show, I needed advertisers, promotions, movie stars and guests, and I had none. I dreamed of Robin Williams but had no way of getting to him. Years later, I met him twice—funny, sweet, talented and humble. His death deeply affected my brother who loved him and watched his movies over and over.

---

[8] What she did as an African-American woman out of Chicago was nothing less than stellar. I saw her before the King Brothers syndicated her and thought they treated her like royalty, by which I mean gold in their pockets.

Still with no big movie stars, I didn't give up. I called a TV journalist on the weekend *Good Morning America* who was a close friend of my stepsister and had married the president of ABC and Cap Cities/ABC. I asked her to help me get an agent. I was 35, with my KTVU comedy demo reel. She helped me get me a top-drawer agent from Ken Lindner & Associates who set up appointments with everyone in town: Jay Leno, E! Entertainment, comedian Howie Mandel who was getting his own late night show and considering a woman sidekick, etc. Everywhere, they all said, "The world isn't ready for a woman in late night." I didn't get one job offer. The agent was dumbfounded. She felt I was original, powerful, funny, glamorous, and had the right look. In fact, she said, "I believe, Marcia, that you could be the first really successful woman in late night."

Every psychic said I would be huge in TV and I wasn't. Joan Rivers had done it, but her success had been limited (because of Johnny Carson, she claimed). The top-drawer agent had done her job, and there was nothing more she could do. Howie Mandel, who like Robin was funny, kind, and humble, ended up going on with no sidekick. I was close to being considered for Jay Leno's *On the Street* reporter, but even with an interview with his producer, I never met Jay. (No talent, or a threat?)

Later, I saw that top agent at a NAPTE meeting and could tell she had given up on me.

Nightly, I turned on the TV to watch Conan O'Brien who had never been on TV and could hardly read the teleprompter. I kept thinking, Why can't I be on national TV and be given the same chance as Conan O'Brien? His ratings were so bad for so long, but he had the backing of Lorne Michaels, creator of *Saturday Night Live*, and finally got great. I'd get great, too, if I had that kind of support.

As I reflect on how often I have been one degree and not six of separation from the top of Hollywood, I can't begin to recount all the stories of how often I was so close, but no one would take a risk on me and my talents. Seven years ago, I met the President of HBO and head of VP of Comedy who liked my tape; they were quite nice to me, but nothing. I met Sean Penn, one of my favorite actors, backstage at the Rolling Stones concert, the LAX Airport lounge, and even ran into him while parking my car at a Malibu parking lot. I even met him and his producer in 1999 at the Starlight Room where I was waitressing after my late night show has been taken off the air. I pitched my late night show to his producer, got a meeting with him at Sean's SF production house, and nothing happened.

As I was traveling the US in 1999 trying to sell my show, the most important story must be told. I got an introduction to the president of Tribune Company at a NAPTE meeting. Tribune at that time had 35 stations (before Netflix and Amazon dominated the field) and was the only way you could have a hit and make millions, unless you were wacky David Letterman that NBC and then CBS paid millions to, or you had Lorne Michaels backing you. But for the 100th time, all the president of Tribune had for me was, "Marcia, you are really talented, but the world is not ready for a woman in late night. It is too much of a risk." Conan O'Brien got the break I didn't get.

I think everyone assumed that because my father was a millionaire, he must be investing in me, and if he wasn't investing in me, why not? If your own father doesn't think you're a good investment, why should anyone else think you are?

My last risk before it was all over was to send my tape to the man in charge of all the ABC stations (and who now runs ABC and Disney), and ask him if he could help me not only with the local ABC SF station but help me to get the national show I dreamed of. (I had also gotten to the head at CBS, but he had passed.) He was very kind in his handwritten note, saying it was up to Joe Ahern and he couldn't get involved. I doubt he had ever even seen the tape. I had met him through my stepsister and have seen him a few times over the years. He has always been humble and kind, despite being the most powerful man in TV. I doubt he even remembers that note. He and his TV journalist wife—the only woman to help me in the entertainment business by introducing me to a top agent—never ask how I am doing when I see them, nor did either of them come to my *Bardo Blues* screening at the La Femme Film Festival. Everyone is busy, and why help me now when I haven't made it in Hollywood, right? When you are famous and powerful, that's what happens. People outside your inner circle always want something from you, and then you are kind if you respond to them, "kind" meaning I am giving you a few minutes of my time. For them, my career had stalled since they never saw me on TV. Pretty savvy assumption.

That was it. My career may have been over in Hollywood terms but not the lingering irony. My show was taken off the air, and I owed the crew $150,000 that I could only pay once the show aired weekly for a year. I had convinced everyone to wait for their check because they believed in me. I ended up having to waitress at the Starlight Room, the bar where my late night show first aired. But even there I was so bad at balancing eight martini glasses on a tray that I was moved to Mama's breakfast place down the street to waitress Tuesday, Wednesday, and Friday while selling leather goods Monday and Thursday. Bills have to be paid one way or another, and my child support check was only enough to cover my San Francisco rent.

Let's face it: The deck is stacked against women making it in late night. When I met comedian Byron Allen, he was doing the exact same thing as I was at the same time with an E! Entertainment alternative Hollywood interview show he sold to 200 stations—like the King brothers, but to African Americans. No one had ever done that, but no woman had done what I was trying to do, either. I'll never forget how he recognized that I was a single mother and couldn't keep nonstop cross-country selling. Byron is now worth $500 million; his company Entertainment Studios owns Freestyle, the distributor for my *Bardo Blues*. More irony, huh?

# 5

# Powerlessness and Fathers

What a happy child my brother Graham was, so loved by my father and stepmother and his three sisters! As my mother's golden child, I sometimes resented Graham for being our dad's golden child, and yet Graham—my beloved brother and years later my best friend—spent half his life in enough torment to drive him to suicide at 48.

I remember the day in Dad's perfect bachelor pad living room in San Francisco when he said, "Marcia, you're in denial about your brother. He was picked up at the airport, talking to himself like someone who had lost his mind." Then he handed me the book *How A Family Deals With Mental Illness*, promising it would help me understand Graham's diagnosis.

The whole scene is nailed into my memory, from the crescent couch the size of four couches—so that at every angle you couldn't miss the Golden Gate Bridge out the panoramic window—to my father's frightening, powerful, charismatic presence that made me drift away so I couldn't hear his painful words.

I stared at the Bay, playing with the purple and yellow pillows a designer had chosen, wondering if Graham was really mentally ill or an artist and oracle like the ones in Delphi in 1400 BCE, too sensitive for 21st century America. My father was again divorced and labeling his child who didn't fit the mold chosen for him. The truth was that Graham was smarter and wiser than anyone in our family but still had to stand in the shadow of the icon boutique hotelier whose only clue about being a good father was keeping poverty at bay by making a lot of money. Was Graham just on overload from all the dimensions pouring through his portals of consciousness? I hear from the dead now and then, but if Emanuel Swedenborg was right, Graham heard from them 24/7. How does one hear voices of the dead 24 hours a day like Swedenborg and not go crazy?

I remember wondering if my father was thinking of how he'd repeated his own abandonment by his mother and father with his own children. What I wanted to say to him was, "Who wouldn't lose their mind, if they were your child?"

Clinical psychologist Louise Hayes' definition of mental illness is "breaking away from the family." That sounds right, at least as regards our family. But fighting with Bill Kimpton required the armor of Joan of Arc (who, by the way, had long conversations with the Archangel Michael, Saint Margaret and Saint Catherine, for which she was locked up and then burned at the stake), and when you lost and were splattered all over the battlefield, the Humpty Dumpty of your mind and soul was racing to the bar to forget.

"Dad, do the doctors think it's because he took LSD?"

He shrugged. "Statistics say schizophrenia can occur from LSD. Others think it's genetic."

My voice rose a decibel. "They're labeling him schizophrenic? Genetic from whom? Grandma? So don't question diagnoses or doctors?" Psychiatrists follow the Diagnostic and Statistical Manual of Mental Disorders like lemmings.

Dad always said I was so much like his mother, and he thought she was undiagnosed bipolar. My stepmother's grandfather had been an eccentric painter who could have been mentally ill. Was what Graham was going through genetic? Once again, I felt powerless before my father's pronouncement.

Graham had grown up in San Francisco with my father, stepmother, and her daughter from her previous marriage who was later awarded the Pulitzer. In elementary, middle and high school, Graham was the popular star athlete with Dad's movie star looks who excelled in everything but academics. He avoided studying for tests but read tons, understood Sartre and existentialism, and pondered the meaning of life. His observations on humanity were brilliantly funny and way over our father's head, for which Dad labeled him Most Likely Not To Succeed, just as he had been labeled. (In eighth grade, I was voted Most Likely To Succeed, but what exactly is "success," and would you recognize it?) Sadly, Graham lacked the self-esteem to value his own uniqueness as well as the self-guidance to pursue making something out of all he perceived and knew.

When his mother and our father divorced, he was 12 years old and deeply affected by going from a constant (if not constantly happy) family life to living between two homes. Dad abandoned Graham as he had abandoned my sister and me after his first divorce by throwing himself into developing his Kimpton Hotel Group and getting caught up in the usual divorce fallout of partying and sleeping around. Graham joined the rest of us (including our father) suffering from terrible depression. I didn't even know depression was a diagnosis until I was 18 and heading into therapy at my father's request. No one had ever asked me, "How are you feeling, Marcia?"

When he was 23, Graham took LSD at Joshua Tree National Park and opened the portals of heaven and hell. Our conversations turned to questioning the American reality we were confronted with, and how one could be true to one's own life under such conditions. Graham saw beyond the mortal flesh and into the deep mind of reality where form began, but had to face the loneliness of never finding friends who also agonized over this modern existential dilemma.

"They're out there, Graham," I assured him, though I hadn't a clue how he might find such rare gems. Mensa? Esalen? Run an ad? I hadn't a clue.

"No, Marcia, mark my words: people think I'm crazy."

"You aren't crazy, Graham, you just see more than most people."

In his 30's he realized he was an artist, but either because of Dad's success, or his mother representing artists in her gallery, but not her son's work, or his sister winning the Pulitzer, Graham never felt worthy of success, whereas I felt worthy of succeeding even if the worldly definition eluded me. I never compared my art to anyone else's because each artist has her or his own unique vision. Graham compared himself constantly, and his three sisters' admiration of his brilliance could not save him.

I visited him at the UCSF Medical Center that felt like a prison. Other than being born, it was his first time in a hospital. An attendant buzzed me in through the first door, asked my name, then buzzed me through a second shiny one-foot thick door like a bank safe. But it wasn't millions of dollars in cash or gold waiting on the other side; it was my brother lying on a bed with a blank Thorazine stare, lost and with no way out of the sudden world of lockdown doors and chemical lobotomies, good intentions be damned. Inside his drugged mind, he is trying to get out as voices and spirits attempt to contact him, or was it a combination of a chemically imbalanced brain picking up on dead people all day long? Later, after studying Swedenborg and his experiences of hearing spirits from heaven and hell, I will wonder about those spirits. Were they good or bad?

"How are you, Graham?"

"OK."

"What've you been doing?"

"Watching TV."

Until his death, my brother bonded with TV as a means of shutting out the voices all his medications couldn't block.

When we went to Greece for two weeks in 2006, we had fun, but it was hard on him not to have a television to escape into, other than the three channels discussing Michael Jackson's recent death day and night at the remote Santorini hotel we stayed in.

Had it been foreshadowing?

When I learned that he heard voices all day long, my denial system thought It can't be. At first, I thought it was the voices of our multilevel ego we all hear as we struggle with life, like I shouldn't have said that or Why am I losing my hair? etc. Biologist Bruce Lipton talks about voices of cellular memories—maybe it was that. But Graham was hearing threats from the postman, the guy in line at the grocery store, the CIA, and people he didn't know. What did it mean?

In the UCSF Medical Center dayroom, I stared at the medicated men staring at the television and felt the sense of unreality that my brother was starring in *One Flew Over the Cuckoo's Nest*, the movie he watched many times out of his fear that, like McMurphy, he would eventually be pharmaceutically lobotomized and locked out of his life forever. Graham and I had nothing to say to each other, and it was heartbreaking. His blue eyes were rimmed in black from all the drugs. Nothing will ever be the same again, I said to myself. The part of his mind the doctors claimed to be trying to heal was wandering in a desert far from Joshua Tree. I will never forget that blank stare, as if he knew he was trapped by some outside or inside force. My brother and best friend was gone, and I could only hope he would magically return.

Once he was moved from the West Coast to the East Coast's "best" psychiatric hospital, Harvard McClean, there was no going back.[9] My San Francisco family were basically

---

[9] Mental Health America, "Position Statement 22": "…involuntary treatment should only occur as a last resort and should be limited to instances where persons pose a serious risk of physical harm to themselves or others in the near future and to circumstances when no less restrictive alternative will respond adequately to the risk. For involuntary treatment to be used, stringent procedural safeguards and fair and regular review are essential."

intelligent people who boiled "crazy" down to somehow not playing by the rules, the penalty being ending up on a conveyor belt of hospitals, doctors, and drugs. Graham was condemned to negotiate whatever term the shrinks came up with for whatever was going on in his brain that they didn't really understand. Isolated in Boston despite visits from his mother and sister, medicated and left alone for days and weeks at a time, Graham went from being a magical, special human being with amazing artistic talent to a tragedy for whom suicide appeared to be the only option that could ease his suffering and sorrow. Eventually, he was able to live for years on his own, but the voices never left him. I am fully convinced that by then, he'd already been left alone in his mind way too long with the wrong drugs.

For 25 years, Graham asked me, "When will this stop, Marcia? " I pray it has now stopped for him in what I believe is heaven.

Will I end up like my brother? I had a typical fall-apart divorce nervous breakdown due to the death of my family dream and was for a time trapped in a desert of depression and recriminations, questioning everything I thought I had known. But Graham's suffering took place in a much darker, deeper no-man's-land. Even the hell of divorce has upsides, but Graham's hell was like his favorite movie in his DVD player the night he committed suicide— *Apocalypse Now* (1979) with Marlon Brando playing Colonel Kurtz ("The horror, the horror")—with no upside in sight. Sedation ("balance") for such a brilliant mind meant wandering further and further from his natural beaten path.

My meditation teacher Gary Springfield has spoken many times about how the memories of wounds remain in our cells and psyche until their energy configuration is unwound and healed. Once the memories become part of us, only we can resolve and release them. As a child, I felt that I couldn't escape; deep down, I still feel I can't, though I'm equally determined no one will entrap me again. No one can take my joy away, because as a divine being, I am fully supported by the universe. And so I write this book to tell my story to see what it can tell me and others. Why else write a book? Stirring up painful memories allows us the opportunity to release and heal them, and to measure how far we've come.

Regarding the family life that shaped Graham and me, I think of what Abraham Lincoln said about our entire nation just before the Civil War erupted: *A house divided against itself cannot stand.*

I was eight when Graham was born. He was brought up in San Francisco while I was brought up in Chicago. In a sense, my father's and stepmother's home in San Francisco seemed more peaceful, though during my visits I could always feel the undertow of an invisible power struggle producing loneliness around every corner. This was what Graham lived with.

In Chicago, my childhood was basically happy, and yet all I remember is unhappiness. Why? Master Tom in Japan taught me that how we are born affects our entire life. Following 1961 accepted hospital practices, my mother was "put under" and I was pulled out with a forceps, after which nurses left me to scream in my hospital bassinet and taught my mother to let me scream at home. In other words, my abandonment began even before generational patterns began to shape me.

My mother didn't drink much while pregnant with me, but she always smoked, which is partially why I believe I have asthma to this day. Chinese medicine would say that my lungs hold the emotion of grief like the liver holds anger. In college I studied smoking mothers and the effects on embryos and came to the conclusion that I began feeling my mother's anxiety in utero—anxiety she would calm with a cigarette. So I was born incapable of breathing properly and filled with her anxiety. In her defense, my mother was only doing what everyone else was doing. Like my father and stepfather, she did better than her mother and father had done. That's how the generational

Bardo works, right? Incremental improvements to what you inherited sight unseen and grew up with.

My namesake grandmother's tragic death by fire in 1962, my parents' divorce in 1965, my questionable babysitter while my mother taught at a South Side public school, my father leaving when I was three-and-a-half and seeing him just once a week until he moved to San Francisco in 1969 and then three times a year from then on—all of it fed into the generational abandonment theme. But I have managed to improve on my original inheritance. I too chase the dream of success like my father, but did not abandon my daughter to do it. Regarding my mother's "golden child" projection onto me of what she hadn't been able to accomplish, I have made the confidence that I can do anything and everything I set my sights on into a buffer against the powerlessness my father passed on to me.

After marrying in 1967, my mother and stepfather Ray Short struggled admirably to balance family life with four kids from two marriages, and yet a lot slipped beyond their purview. Years later, my youngest sister finally confessed that a relative had sexually abused her when she was seven. I feel confident it didn't happen to me, but who knows? Do my issues with powerlessness and men include this, too? Compound blended family chaos with a family predator and a stepfather going through the stress of starting his own business, and what level of chaos do you have?

In the 1970's suburbs, everyone drank like on the show *Mad Men* (2007-2015). Drinking looked glamorous on TV, and my parents had fun parties to the beat of Neil Diamond and Pink Floyd. Block parties often meant rampant alcohol-driven affairs far beyond a couple of glasses of wine after tennis doubles. Both my father and stepfather limited martini lunches to Fridays because both were ambitious entrepreneurs starting their own companies and wanted a clear head for business, but when the day was over, the wine at home ran like a fountain of oblivion.

Spanking was also then in vogue. Fortunately, my father only spanked me once, whereas my Chicago parents spanked liberally, years later rationalizing that everyone spanked, your stepbrother (from my stepfather's first marriage) was difficult, etc. The spectrum from spanking to hitting to beating has never been clear to me. I never spanked my daughter and don't believe such a violent reaction to a child learning boundaries is acceptable. Today, the "spankings" I witnessed my stepbrother undergo would be called abuse. In centuries past, parents viewed their beloved children as possessions and drove them to dysfunction, excusing it with various versions of Proverbs 13:24: *He that spareth his rod hateth his son: but he that loveth him chasteneth him betimes.* My stepbrother "acted out" in part because of being bullied at school for being gay (which none of us knew for years) and then having to come home and sit through martini and wine dinners filled with quarreling. Blamed and beaten repeatedly for basically being a sensitive child acting out in a chaotic household, he eventually contemplated suicide that either I was able to talk him out of or, unlike Graham's, his medication worked. With me, the chaos went inside and eventually added to my sense of powerlessness and self-destructive depression.

Depression as a lifestyle began in earnest in college when I started getting stoned. In the beginning, marijuana lifted my spirits, but I am 100 percent convinced that it led to worse depression by chemically changing me. I finally got off it when I moved to New York City at 25 years old. In LA, I had needed to suppress my mind and make coffee for the predatory Fox GM. Moving to New York meant using my mind again.

I feel guilty writing this because I know my Chicago parents did the best they could, given that they, like everyone else, were subject to *le jeu de la vie* (the game of life aka Bardo) as they had learned it. They loved and supported me in the light they had then by attending my growing-up rites of passage and providing me with a great education. But the truth is that deep inside, I was miserable at home. This book is about breaking free of Bardos, so Marcia Kimpton's truth must be spoken.

Such are the burdens we inherit or create. A big question for me has been how to transcend or work through the emotions I don't want to carry around or feel, as whatever I feel consciously or unconsciously vibrates beyond me like a movie until I finally take responsibility for editing out the parts that don't serve my destiny, loving more deeply the parts that do, and all not through denial and rules, but by transmuting pain and suffering into joy and peace. If you feel powerless, how do you empower yourself? If you feel rejected, how do you keep from rejecting yourself (or finding someone to do it for you)? One meditates. Did that today. Exercise. Did that today. Pray. Did that today. Go into the feeling so deep that it releases. I am trying.

# 6

# From Fathers to Men

In the generational Bardo, fathers and daughters can be as treacherous a territory steeped in illusions and pain as fathers and sons. My father bequeathed bad male modeling to me, so it should be no surprise that I have been wandering single and unsuccessful in my career and in relationships with men. Still, I had some nice years in between with Andrew Moore, a younger man, me 38 and him 25. In fact, Andrew leads straight back to my father's death.

Everything went horribly wrong after my dream late night show was kicked off the air in 1998. Without the Budweiser ad money, I had to pay the crew with my one-time lump sum child-support settlement of $150,000. When I didn't have enough to pay my director Jesse, he kindly agreed to wait a while. No more child support meant my two jobs—waitressing and selling leather outfits at a top-end leather goods store—would have to cover my bills going forward. I believed I could pay Jesse over time. He was patient for a while, but eventually (1) couldn't believe I didn't have the money, despite having seen me waitressing at Mama's breakfast place one morning, and (2) probably thought that if I didn't have the money, my rich father did and would pay, if not for his daughter, at least to avoid a scandal.

The last time I saw my dad before his final hospitalization was Christmas in Palm Springs. In fact, that was the first Christmas he'd personally picked out our Christmas gifts instead of just handing us a check. (He gave me a book about Princess Diana, whom I loved.) He was so damned grateful to be alive and so present—like people are just before they die, though I do believe he thought he was going to live—that he was like a different father. He had beaten everything in his life—abandonment, physical abuse, dyslexia, poverty, two divorces—so of course he was going to beat cancer. His best friend had also been diagnosed with leukemia and recovered, so of course Dad wasn't going to die eight months after his diagnosis. Perhaps having a young third wife with double-D boobs made him truly believe the odds were with him.

The entire family was together and it was beautiful, except that we were in un-Christmas-like Palm Springs. I stayed Christmas Eve, then flew back to San Francisco to be with my daughter on Christmas Day when my ex handed her off. Before leaving, I asked Dad if I could help when he flew to Houston once a month for his chemo treatments, but he said no. It was heartbreaking that he wouldn't let me help, and that Isabel, the woman he chose to marry and help him, had nothing in common with him.

"Marcia, she just doesn't understand the language fully."Isabel was Swedish.

"She doesn't understand that cats like fish, either, Dad. The Dane I fell in love with at least understood that."

"You're not very tolerant of people."

I shut up right there. Dad couldn't hear that I wanted to be close to him. I hugged him, told him I loved him, and left.

A month later, as I was walking across a San Francisco park near my small apartment, I was served papers by Jesse's lawyer. To top it off, Jesse was suing my father along with me, and when the papers were served on my father, he had to be rushed in the express medical transporter to the hospital. Immediately, I regretted not having given Jesse the monthly $500 he'd asked for. I had fallen for the illusion that stardom was just around the corner as I sent my late night show out to agents and TV stations, and that I would pay Jesse in one grand gesture. But it was over; no one wanted my show, I was broke, and my father wouldn't give me a loan. Dad sent me a letter informing me that his doctor advised it was too stressful for him to think about the lawsuit, so I was not to see him while he was in the hospital. Those were the rules, and no one broke Bill Kimpton's rules, not even a daughter.

My sister was furious with me; the stress of the lawsuit was my fault, and I would never see my father again. When I asked if I might visit while Dad could still sit upright and crack jokes from his cancer bubble about how he wanted the original Swenson's ice cream from San Francisco and not the Houston franchise, my sisters avoided answering, because they wanted to abide by Bill Kimpton's rules.

That night, I drank too much in the Starlight Room on the roof of the Kimpton Hotel where I had had my late night show a few years before. My soon-to-be boyfriend Andrew was bartending that night.

"I'll have a starlight lemon drop," I sulked.

"How are you doing?" he asked. "You're not looking too good."

"Dad is dying and I can't see him."

"What?"

"Remember when you were making the drinks and my late night show went off the air? What you didn't know was that I still owe my director Jesse, whose lawsuit claims that I owe him $8,000 per day for the eight days of filming because that was what we agreed."

"But you don't have the money, right?"

"He thinks I have money, but why would I waitress at Mama's if I had money? Even here, you helped me keep my waitress job, despite my spilling so many drinks."

"So he wants $64,000, and Budweiser didn't even pay you."

"Right. He's suing me and my father, and now I can't visit Dad in the hospital where he's dying because of all the stress the lawsuit has caused him."

"I thought your dad was a great guy."

"He is—to employees."

"Someone told me he's worth $110 million. Can't he help you?"

"Apparently not. Can I have another lemon drop?"

He started making the drink. "What are you going to do?"

"Drink until I don't feel it."

The Starlight roof bar got busy as it did every night, and I was soon talking to two cute Frenchmen. I really liked Andrew, but our age difference made me think we would never hook up. I drank and drank until one of the Frenchmen slurred, "What are you doing tonight?"

"Drinking with you."

"Want to do anything else?"

Being single for years after my divorce meant not meeting the right men in San Francisco and not a lot of sex unless you count fucking around with one-night stands every six months when the loneliness got really bad. Of course, one-night stands are generally saturated with alcohol and as far from love as you can get, so I rarely felt great the next morning. This night, however, there was the lawsuit that had sent my father to the hospital, he was dying, and I was never going to see him again, so I said to myself, What the fuck? Why not a *ménage à trois* with two gorgeous Frenchmen?

I went downstairs to the Kimpton Hotel, rented a discounted room, and returned to the bar. "I've got the key," I informed the Frenchmen.

"We've got the rest," they smiled.

The next morning I woke with one of the worst hangovers ever and was on fragile mental ground. My daughter was with her father and I wasn't working that day, so I called my brother-in-law.

"Len, I'm losing my mind—literally, no joke. Get me into my dad's fucking hospital room."

"I can't do that, Marcia, you know the drill."

"Well, I know my brother has nothing to do with this, so tell my sisters and Isabel that I'm on the razor's edge. I feel like I'm going to kill myself if I don't get to say goodbye to the man I have loved all my life."

"Marcia, you are not going to kill yourself."

"You're right—I can't do that to my daughter. I live for her, not for family that don't help me while my father is dying. I wanted a successful TV show and family and instead I have a beautiful daughter I can only see half time. I didn't want to be alone, Len. My dream is ruined. Tell me what the fuck I should live for."

I look around the hotel room. The Kimpton name is everywhere—the pens, the pad of paper next to the phone, the menu—even the yoga mat in the corner has Kimpton taped around it—and yet I'm not allowed to see the man who created all of this because my career, marriage, and life are a failure in his mind.

Len says he'll do everything he can and hangs up.

Apparently, Isabel was able to override my sisters to get me in to see Dad barely in time. Dad and Isabel had been together for four years. After his cancer diagnosis, they had married so no one would think she was just another daughter, given that she was younger than I. The logic of giving her the same last name as his daughters escaped me, but there it was. He'd met her at the Hoffman Process spiritual retreat center where she was a masseuse. Dad said they had just "hit it off," but whatever the story was, I was grateful to Isabel because I was at last at my father's side and looking into the face of the most important man in my life. Once a hotel icon with hair so full it waved like Elvis's, Dad was fading away along with his hair, movie star teeth and smile, and athletic six-pack. His hamstrings from running six miles a day now hung from his bones, and his mouth was pursed around tubes running down his throat to help him breathe. The old Paul Newman eyes were shut, due to the sedation for the breathing tube. *This must be what death looks like*, I thought, and then felt guilty for thinking it.

Our last moments together, his hand quivered. "Dad, may Buddha and Jesus Christ be with you as you transition," I whispered, "I am so sorry for going broke, and I am so sorry for this lawsuit. Please say hello to my grandmother Marcia Kimpton."

Yellow was Dad's favorite color.

When was it that Dad's secretary Marianne called?"We've transferred money into your account and booked a flight for tomorrow."

"Who told you to do this?"

"Your father said if he was close to death, this is what should happen for all his children."

I fell to my knees. "Thank you, Marianne."

It's over, he's dead, I thought, they pulled the plug and I wasn't there.

My daughter cried for days and nights. I had never seen her cry like this. In fact, I'd never known the impact her grandfather had had on her until that moment.

While we planned the funeral, my stepsister said she didn't want me to speak at the funeral.

"Why, Jenny? How can you say that when he is my father?"

"Because—"

"No, there is no because. You don't have the right to tell me I can't speak at my father's funeral. I'm paying the price for his death. Let me get up in front of a thousand people and tell them all Dad was my biggest teacher.—And thank you, Jenny, for your connections at the New York Times and getting his obit in it."

Three days before the funeral, we Skyped with the trustees in San Francisco who asked us to read the will with two lawyers in the room. Dad was worth $110 million, of which he left Isabel a large chunk.

"Bob and Barry," Isabel beseeched, "I really need help since Bill's death."

"Sure, what can we do, Isabel?"

"Help me get to the Wells Fargo Bank?"

That must have been a showstopper for the trustees who probably looked at each other. "We can get someone to help you there, but we're in San Francisco."

"OK, but I don't know how to get there."

My brother and two sisters—Dad had adopted my stepsister when she was 18 to make sure there was no question about her being his daughter, too—directly inherited, but I was to be subject to trustees controlling my trust.

I was in shock that Dad had changed the will on my birthday. I was also in shock that he had left me money and that I might be OK for the rest of my life. Wow.

Given how many men and women we meet in a lifetime, it is remarkable, isn't it, how few of them really impact our lives. Why so few? For me, the men who have deeply impacted me have in one way or another had to do with unresolved issues around my father. It may sound trite, but all roads lead to Rome until childhood parent issues become conscious enough to be resolved. Even if we try to choose men or women as unlike dear old dad or mom as possible, they end up being like them. The chemistry of it all is pretty mystical. Our unconscious puzzle pieces seem to go around looking for their match. So far, I've talked about my relationships with TV general managers and producers, my once true love now my ex-husband, and my longtime mental affair with Mick Jagger. Parts of my father were etched into each one of them, whether under the theme of domination, degradation, or impossible stardom.

Just one healthy, sane man stands out as not being a Dad puzzle piece. Jim and I dated for three years back in our college days. The love and acceptance between us seemed almost effortless, but he was sane, strong, smart, and stable—a wonderful catch, as women say—which is probably why I didn't marry him. The unconscious me was more interested in complex, unresolved, impossible abusive relationships loaded with father material.

At IU, Jim's love of accomplishment and the commitment it takes to do the work that real, lasting accomplishment requires ended in him winning the Wells Senior Recognition Award for "excellence in academic achievement and excellence of contribution to the campus community through leadership and participation in campus activities." Jim didn't even take the time to meet me for lunch sex—probably the only guy on campus too busy to have sex with his girlfriend.

At one point after we'd both graduated, I moved to London to live with him just after I'd broken up with the deadhead guy who actually stalked me all the way to London.

He buzzed our flat and said to me, "I'm downstairs, please meet me for coffee."

I couldn't believe it. He lived in faraway LA. "You can't be downstairs."

"I am. I want to talk to you and you won't talk to me, so I'm here."

"It's been five months and I'm living with Jim. You live in LA." He couldn't be downstairs.

But there he was. Upon seeing him in the teashop, I remembered why I had broken up with him and never wanted to see another Grateful Dead concert. (Together, we had seen 45.) I was done with him and the Dead.

"I had to see where you lived," he said, as if that justified stalking me.

"How did you find out where I lived?"

"I just did. I've been following you for three days."

That definitely frightened me. "You can't do that to women."

"It was my only choice. I bought a gun, took it to the Santa Monica pier and decided not to kill myself, so I'm here in London. I need help, Marcia. I can't get over you."

I finally convinced him that I simply couldn't help him. With more compassion than fear at that point, I said goodbye and watched him trudge over London Bridge. Jim and I had also had a chemical beginning and he too had refused to give up, but he hadn't stalked me.

Nine years later, I was stalking someone I couldn't get over. (Was there some sort of abandonment pattern here?)

I was 34 when I met Kristian at a NATPE (National Association of Television Program Executives) TV conference in New Orleans. He was a Danish TV sales agent and buyer from Denmark, so from day one I knew that we couldn't actually be together because I was a single mother who couldn't chase love to another country. Mind you, I badly wanted love, but I couldn't abandon my daughter like my father had abandoned me.

In part because Kristian represented a hopeless love (like my father), I fell madly and immediately in love with him. He could read my mind, finish my sentences, had a wicked sense of humor, and was physically what I had envisioned all my life: tall, blond, with luminous crystal blue eyes. He made me feel safe. I could lean on him because he didn't mind how strong I was as a woman but mentally and physically enjoyed the challenge.

After the second day of the New Orleans conference, we met at his hotel for a romantic dinner. When he grabbed my hand, it tingled and I knew I would marry him. My ex-husband had grabbed my hand in the same way and produced the same tingle that said, This is the man, signifying that Fate (or was it magical thinking?) was locking me into my pattern: ecstatic joy that would eventually descend into pure hell.

It may seem absurd to call a man I only knew a few days the love of my life, but that was the impact Kristian had on me. It was the first time I really believed in past lives, even that we had been married before. Call me delusional or spellbound, but there were just too many things he had right about me.

Our second night together, his kiss on my cheek, his hand sliding up under my shirt to my breasts, his eyes the lightest blue I have ever seen looking straight into my eyes made me want to feel everything with him. While we were making love, he asked, "Will you marry me?"

"Yes," I said without hesitation.

"Will you marry me?" he said again.

"Yes," I promised again.

Then what had happened to me so many times with men happened: this big confident man's penis started going soft on me. I had actually become used to it. In the beginning I didn't understand it, but later I realized that even the strongest of men went weak before my feminine power. Kristian was strong on the outside, but as far as real strength . . .

After we had finished making love, he went into the bathroom and brought out my birth control pills.

"Why are you taking them?"

"Because I don't want a baby, and we should be having protected sex. I never have sex without a condom."

"I want you to stop taking them."

"What?"

"I want a baby with you."

"Let's first get married."

"OK, let's go to Las Vegas."

The next night of the conference I had a dinner date with Quincy Jones, one of the greatest producers and musicians I've ever met. I'd met him when he was selling his TV show at the Sony conference booth and he'd invited me to dine with his high-roller friends. When I got into his limo, they were all passing the pipe, but I'd wanted to keep my cool and so had passed it on. All night long, we all got in and out of his limo. Now in New Orleans, Quincy had finally asked me for a serious dinner date, but I had met the love of my life.

I told Kristian that I'd call and ask Quincy if he could come along.

"Tell him we are engaged," Kristian said.

"Right, the man I met two days ago."

When I asked Quincy if I could bring a friend, his response was, "Ahh... sure." Later, I realized he thought I was bringing the beautiful woman friend I'd brought along the night we met.

When I hung up, Kristian said he had something to tell me. His blue eyes penetrating me, he said, "The night we met, I was out with my business partner because I didn't feel like being with the model I had flown in and gotten a hotel room for."

"What?"

"I wasn't dating her, it was casual."

"But I was with you that night and tonight. You asked to marry me!"

"I know. When I met you, I told her to go home and she left."

I felt bad for the woman he had dumped, but what he said was alarming. After asking me to marry him on the first night, here was warning sign number two, but I was so in love that I couldn't see the warning signs for what they were. Impulsive (especially in wounded areas) and intuitive (except in wounded areas), I felt like I had found an old friend who had been missing for years or even lifetimes.

It was a strange dinner: me, two tall white Danish men (Kristian and his business partner), and a short black man with an amazing resume. The color difference didn't mean much to Kristian and me, but I think Quincy felt the Viking sexual dynamics. At 37, I was still incredibly naïve. Quincy was dead quiet during dinner while Kristian and I plied him with questions.

The following year while rehearsing for Dick Clark's American Music Awards at the Shriner Auditorium in LA, my first and only time on network TV, I saw Quincy again. I was the behind-the-scenes comedy reporter, and Quincy was there to receive an award. I thought we could do dinner again, but he informed me that that was not going to happen.

"When I ask you on a date, you don't bring along two men." He had viewed my behavior as a power play and slap in the face.

"I didn't think of it as a date, Quincy. I knew you had a girlfriend."

"I didn't have a girlfriend in New Orleans, Marcia, only in LA."

With Hollywood men, it's a girl in every city.

Six years later, I interviewed Quincy for CBS *This Morning*, but it never aired. That was the last time I saw him.

Over the three occasions Kristian and I met during the next year—four days each at two NAPTE conferences in 1998 and 1999, and three days at the MIPTV conference in Cannes—including a few days every other year until five years ago, Kristian must have asked me 20 times to have a child. My answer was always no, though truthfully, I secretly wanted a child with him so bad that I thought I heard a female spirit say she was coming through the next time we met.

To this day when I think of Kristian, I see the scene in the hotel room during the 1999 NAPTE conference in New Orleans. My face is slammed up against the bed frame and Kristian is thrusting his dick over and over into my mouth as his semen gives me no choice but to swallow. I don't mind swallowing a man's spirit in physical form if I am madly in love with him—and I was delirious about Kristian—but I could tell that something was very wrong: We were no longer always laughing, and he was no longer ripping my clothes off with the passion of seven months before at the big MIPTV conference in Cannes, France.

Once he was done coming, he jumped off the bed and started pulling his pants on.

"What are you doing?" I asked. "Is this only a one-way street today?"

My dream man said, "I am in love with another woman."

"What?"

My stomach lurched and I could barely keep myself from running to the bathroom and throwing up. The first thing I heard in my head was It's my fault. Where does that kind of thinking come from? You guessed it: from little Marcia bent on pleasing Daddy so he will love her.

I finally managed, "Well, goodbye, mister," and I jumped out of the bed he'd just jumped out of.

His blue eyes were translucent with anger as he blocked me. "Don't think you are in control of everything, Marcia, and don't think you are the only one."

Even before I got so deeply involved with Kristian, the San Francisco psychic had seen it all: that Kristian and I were soul mates, but because he lived in Denmark and I lived in New York, we would be forced apart and there would be another woman.

"He isn't in love with her like he is with you," the psychic clarified, "but his focus is on work and she is perfect to fill in what he needs to accomplish his goals. He can't wait for you."

Deep down, I wasn't worried about the other woman because the feeling between Kristian and me couldn't be easily replaced. After all, he'd asked to marry me. How, then, could he announce he was in love with someone else? When you meet at a conference and drink beers and dance on Bourbon Street all night, and then at dawn he asks you to marry him over and over, isn't that less a sign of true love more than a sign that all is not as it appears? By 6 am, I'd agreed to marry him and was in his bed, at which point I think I blacked out and had unprotected sex (but was at least on the pill—I was determined to not have abortions). Had I gotten pregnant, I would have had his baby because I wanted a second child and wanted it with him. Every time I saw him, he asked for a baby, but I certainly wasn't going to share him with other women.

All signs, right? I missed them all.

"Marcia, he's a misogynist and will never be monogamous," the San Francisco psychic explained years later. "True, he shattered your heart and it has taken you 22 years to heal, but you will find love," she promised. "The original man who abandoned you was your father. You have to learn to work on your sadness and emptiness by yourself. That is your journey. Once you become your inner child's mother and father, she will be healed and the right man will walk into your life. Forget about Kristian."

I heard her loud and clear but didn't want to believe her, and yet only a misogynist could pull his dick out of my mouth and say in the next breath, "I am in love with another woman."

Next to my daughter, I loved Kristian more than anyone. Even in retrospect at 56, I can say with certainty that I have never felt that kind of consuming love since. I've searched, hoped, and given up, though lately I've been feeling hopeful again that a soul mate—if they exist—may be just around the corner. (But then, what about being able to count on one hand the really happy marriages and partnerships I've seen?)

I wish I'd listened to the San Francisco psychic about forgetting Kristian. But then my higher self maintains that It takes as long as it takes. It's true that most people never figure out how to heal the past, but when Kristian zipped up his pants and prepared to depart 20 years ago, he also zipped up a Hazmat suit around my heart so no one could touch it. The only progress I've made is that when I'm alone, I don't feel alone—or have I just gotten used to feeling alone? Has meditation made me feel the loneliness less? Maybe.

The hellish part has been to forget and forgive both my ex-husband and Kristian. I had a child with my ex-husband, which basically locked me into his movie for 18 years. With Kristian, it was more like being locked into a movie rerun. There is no other way to explain it.

When I finally realized I was losing Kristian, I flew to France for the next big TV conference, faxing Kristian that I was coming to Cannes and would give him a call when I arrived. Like a maniac, I flew into Paris, rented a car, and drove to Cannes instead of flying. (I needed a car because I couldn't find a last minute hotel and would have to stay out of town.) I called him. He said he would call me back but didn't. It was one of the worst, most torturous nights ever. All night, I could hear Michael Sembello singing "Maniac" somewhere.

First thing in the morning, I called Kristian. When he didn't pick up, I called the apartment rental number he'd given me. He answered.

"We've got to meet because I'm leaving."

"Don't leave. Let's meet at the café, Marcia . . ."

Behind his sunglasses, he was an emotional wreck. The strong man who didn't fall apart when his father walked out on his mother and moved in with another woman down the street was falling apart. The wrecked and wounded child who ran his relationships with women was the exact counterpart to my wrecked and wounded child running mine with men. His wounded child was now wounding mine.

"You blew me off last night. You left the woman you said you wanted to marry stranded."

"I am sorry, Marcia."

"I am leaving."

The big Viking Dane was shaking as he grabbed my hand. "Don't leave," he pleaded in a low, sad voice, "we'll figure something out. Let's get together tonight after my meetings."

He loved me, the 6,000 miles between us be damned.

I knew he was dating someone else, but I didn't feel that I was betraying her so much as she was betraying me. Later, I found out her name was Holly—yet another Holly betraying me. The only two men I have truly loved, my ex-husband and Kristian, both ended up with a Holly. Go figure.

Holly, Hollywood, Holy? Had Kristian also asked Holly to marry him? It was impossible.

Later, we met for a drink and talked and laughed. I foolishly assumed it meant that we were getting back together and would make love all night with him throwing me into this position and that like he did in New Orleans. But he became quiet and forlorn: Our easy talk and laughter had been about saying goodbye. He wasn't going to move to San Francisco with his ten employees, and I wasn't moving to Denmark with my daughter.

Suddenly, he said, "My stomach aches, let's meet tomorrow."

"Do you want to come for the European music awards? I've got a pass."

"Sure."

So we met the following day but couldn't get a seat at the awards. He and his work partner and I ended up sitting next to the bar and watching them on the monitor. Then we drove to Jimmy's, the classic nightclub of the rich and famous in Monaco. Kristian excused himself and when he came back to our table boasted to his work partner and me, "I just touched the breasts of Tyra Banks."

"What?" I couldn't believe he was bragging about Tyra Banks' breasts.

"I passed her on the dance floor and made sure I touched them," he said proudly like a teenager.

Bragging about Tyra Banks shocked me into reality. Why the hell are you with this man? my higher self asked. Who cares if you had a past life with him, you don't want a future life with him.

I stood up and headed for the bathroom. When I returned to our table, I was the little girl whose father hadn't listened to her and now felt abandoned, hurt, and violated. Why didn't I leave? Because the pull of Kristian was the strongest I had ever experienced.

Back at his apartment, we had one of the most passionate lovemaking sessions we'd ever had. When we awoke the next morning, I knew it was the end. The vulnerable little girl hugged the vulnerable little boy. Pop songs insist It'll work out, but he and I knew it wouldn't.

Crying, I left for my hotel room as Ben Harper sang "Another Lonely Day" on a radio somewhere near. I drove back to Paris, then flew to San Francisco and cried and cried at the Golden Gate Bridge. The love of my life, or what I perceived to be the love of my life, was gone. When I called him a few months later, he picked up and barely talked, telling me that Holly was there. I told him I was returning to Europe, to which he said nothing. It was fall in Paris and I'd be seeing a close friend, revisiting an affair with rugby player Jean Pierre Rives, and meeting Johnny Pigozzi, my soon-to-be introduction to Mick Jagger. But it was Kristian I still longed for. I faxed him the dates I'd be in Copenhagen. Once again, no return phone call.

A friend asked why I was going.

"Because I have to know where he lives." Exactly what my stalker had said in London.

"Do you have his address?"

"Not his home but his office address."

"You're stalking him," she said.

I didn't want to see it as stalking. In order to release him from my psyche, I had to go to Copenhagen, the first European city I had flown into at 18.

The plane landed. No one met me at the airport. I checked into a drab hotel. In 1998, there were no beautiful hotels in Copenhagen like there are today. I took a cab to Kristian's office building on the outskirts of Copenhagen. It was Sunday and I knew he worked 80-hour weeks developing his TV sales and distribution company, but he wasn't there. I got out of the cab and hid in the bushes. Frantic, I peered into every first floor window like a serial killer. Like my stalker in London, I wanted Kristian to fill my void and heal my wounds.

I wanted to escape into him, to make a little family with him and pass on everything I am and am not with him. I wanted him to love me and only me.

Stalking someone in the name of love is insanity. Peering into Kristian's office window was about hoping to connect with something, anything of his, but I didn't see anything. He was not there. It was Sunday morning and he was with naked Holly waking up in bed. He knew I was in his town but he never followed up, which meant refusing to see me. I was desperately lonely. Holly wasn't lonely. She was with my man who was her man because he chose her over me.

Six years after Copenhagen, Kristian visited me while pondering leaving Holly. I was dating someone, but he came anyway, even knowing that his strong exterior falls apart around me and that it would be difficult. When I brought up his telling me he had fallen in love with another woman and what it had done to me, he didn't remember. (Not remembering is a way of betraying or abandoning someone.) When I forgave him that night in Napa Valley's St. Helena after talking for hours like I was with my best friend, then said goodbye the next day, I swear Jesus Christ or some magical high vibratory angel visited me in bed and I changed forever. Kristian now has four children with two women. Having been awarded sole custody of three of the four, he has moved to Brazil, leaving his daughter with her mother.

There but for fortune go I.

It is now years later and I am eating greasy chicken wings and drinking my second glass of wine. Can I go deep enough into writing this book that I visit the abyss, the shadow my writing coach talks about, and find the color in the deepest, saddest moment that my other writing coach says is the poetry of life? I am certainly not writing this book to wallow in the pain I'm revisiting and releasing; I would prefer other less invasive ways of release. I am writing this book to show how people can work through and transcend anything in the Earth Bardo, including dark chapters of one's life. All can be alchemized into light and wisdom. I can't bring my brother back, nor can I know why Kristian affected me as he did, but I can make conscious one layer after another. All I see is innate goodness unless someone is dark and on the edge of committing a crime they will regret for the rest of their life. I am still like a child who only sees the good in everyone, the trick being how much of it they can manage to embody and share.

> *Lower ego: Is this how life is? We enter life alone, we die alone . . .*

> *Higher Self: Alone describes the Bardo, not life. Life, real life, is full to overflowing.*

So it is family imprinting that has made it so I can't have love and won't be loved. My father loved me as his offspring but imprinted me with There are many more important things than you, Marcia. From screaming in the crib and no one picking me up, holding or hearing me, to my father not attending my school functions or visiting me at Indiana University (including graduation) because he was busy building his empire, the imprint runs like one of those 3D printers in my cells and blood loaded with abandonment. I have constantly abandoned myself by choosing men who abandon me. Chemically and alchemically, I have been drawn to men like my father who ask to marry me and then are gone.

My father broke my heart, then my ex-husband, then Kristian. My ex-husband's style was to tell me to be a stay-at-home wife, then to yell at me if I forgot to change the light bulb on the front porch. When I finally left, it meant that our one-and-a-half-year-old daughter had to undergo the chaos of divorce with us. Even after I left, I had no control over what he did to her or me. More powerlessness.

The ancestral imprint stops only when I finally wake up and heal it.

*The Lord is longsuffering, and abundant in mercy, forgiving iniquity and transgression; but He by no means clears the guilty, visiting the iniquity of the fathers on the children to the third and fourth generation. (Numbers 14:18)*

I tear into the chicken wing like it's my last. The further into this book I go, the more I tear apart the shadow that no amount of chicken wings and wine will fill. The only thing that will fill it is God's light and love, the Holy Spirit and the Higher Self. Even knowing this, I came straight to the Santa Fe bar where I am now writing.

My one relationship in the 20 years since Kristian was beautiful, and it was with Andrew, whom I introduced earlier in this chapter as my father lay dying. Andrew and I started out in January 2001 when I was waitressing at the Starlight Room after my late night show went off the air, and he was the cute young bartender studying film. Though younger than me by several years, Andrew helped me deal with the fallout of my divorce and later my father's death. I wasn't exactly a prize for a kind, cute, young bartender, what with needing comfort for my custody battle PTSD, my cancelled show, and not being allowed to be at my dying father's side. (Would I ever grow beyond repeating what went on with my parents?)

Another bite of chicken wing and sip of red wine. (It's healthy, right? I don't know where the chicken is from, but I tried to get the best non-arsenic wine.) I thought about the gifted psychic's prediction in 1987: "You are going to become very famous and successful in everything you've dreamed, but it will be when you are much older." I have been living the victim and not the victor, resisting my life's slow plan and only making the chains lock tighter. Every time I feel I'm finally moving forward, the chains tighten and I seek refuge in alcohol and grass to numb the pain of failure. In order to face off the father pattern of rejection by the men who run the Hollywood

Bardo and the abandonment and betrayal by the men I'm drawn to romantically, I must first face off the pattern of turning to alcohol and instead develop the self-discipline of meditation and yoga.

I had forgiven Kristian on St. Helena and soon would forgive my ex-husband for having been far worse to me. Compassion paves the way to forgiveness. No one acts like that toward a woman they claim to love unless they lack love for themselves as well as lack respect for women as real human beings. At the Swedenborg Church, I gave a talk on how forgiveness has released me from the anger eating away at me like a cancer. I spoke about the amazing fact that forgiveness is more about the one who forgives than the ones forgiven because you are dropping burdens so you can ascend the mountain to freedom. Forgiveness changes the forgiver, whereas the one forgiven may or may not choose to change. By forgiving these two men and my father and mother, I release the love that had become hopelessly entangled with anger and resentment so I can once again breathe unfettered.

# 7

# Behind the Scenes of *Bardo Blues*

What it takes to make a film is, first, the person you are. But if that person is a woman with no big Hollywood budget, it might just cost good friends along the way, especially if it seems the stakes are mounting.

I don't know anyone other than myself who has produced an entire film from casting, locations, and schedule to every production detail of costumes, props, catering, etc. My only options were to produce the entire film myself or forget it. I produced my first film *My Reality* for $150,000. With my second film *Bardo Blues*, not only did I not have enough money, but a tax lien was also chasing me. I was 50 when my first film was completed, and by *Bardo Blues* I was 56. In *My Reality*, I acted the most, but by *Bardo Blues* I had learned enough to act less so the pressure on me was less intense. Instead of producing *Bardo Blues* in my hometown of San Francisco, I produced it in northern Thailand. In both films I had a crew of 12, but in Thailand we added six local Thai.

The stress I was under cost me two 30-year friendships going all the way back to Indiana University—one while shooting *My Reality*, the other while shooting *Bardo Blues*.

My old friend Kristen was my partner in creativity and made me laugh more than anyone. When we were both 26, she had held the camera for *Video Dreamers* and created it with me in hopes that we would be on NBC or FOX, as the bidding war then suggested. It was Kristen who had found the nice white male executive producer (essential in 1989) to take *Video Dreamers* to both NBC and FOX. No one had supported me more in my career and helped me to heal my wounds than Kristen. I loved her like a sister and wanted her in my movie and up in San Francisco for my 50th birthday, so I had planned her flight well in advance of filming *My Reality*.

On my way to location on day 3 of producing, directing and acting, she called about some detail having to do with her flight. Of all the people I knew, I assumed Kristen understood the pressure I was under: doing every role in the movie except holding the camera, organizing to get everything done in advance to anticipate problems, etc. (Is it even possible to produce a film without an assistant?) She had always been there for me, so why didn't she know to check the Southwest flight number herself?

Deep into producing the film without an assistant, I blew up.

Maybe it was just the pressure chamber of achieving something as big as an entire film, but it was also true that our long friendship had for some time been heading downward. I don't quite understand why. Maybe we were just evolving in different directions, she a second grade teacher and I a movie producer. However you cut it, I blew up at my breaking point over a simple question.

After she told me over the phone that our 30-year friendship was over, I was able to turn the pathos of losing my best friend into confronting my boss about the dumbing down of TV. Then I did the best acting of my life in the third act of *My Reality*, when the character "Marcia" breaks. At Lee Strasberg, I had been taught to use the real life method inspired by Stanislavski to magnify and intensify my connection to the character's emotional experiences through my own life experiences.

Kristen didn't show up to my 50th birthday party and we did not speak again until I contacted her about her husband's cancer and again six years later regarding Graham's suicide. I asked her to meet me for lunch since we both lived in LA, but she called to say that she was sorry for my loss but was done grieving the loss of our friendship and wouldn't meet me. Once again, I had set up an abandonment. No one has ever quite replaced the beauty and closeness of my friendship with Kristen. Now, my friends Lilli, Shirley and Kat make me laugh.

Maybe such losses are part of being a woman caught in the crosshairs of the Hollywood Bardo, particularly when she never gives up on her dream and therefore unintentionally ends up sacrificing even the people who once supported that dream along the way.

I lost my other old IU friend Gina during *Bardo Blues*. Whereas Kristen had asked about her Southwest flight number after I had sent her all the info well in advance, Gina sent an email asking about laundry facilities at the Thai hotel. I lost it, and it cost me another friend.

Gina had been a struggling actress for 25 years in LA and had moved with her son and actor-theater director-husband to Nashville. I'd given Gina an amazing opportunity to be in her second or third film because she was a great actress and perfect for the role of "Clare" the villain, a much more interesting role than mine as the angel "Gabrielle." I flew her in for auditions for the lead and rehearsals and hired her husband Mark to coach the lead Stephen McClintic into an award-winning performance (26 awards and counting). Mark did all the prep work so Stephen could be perfect on set, which is why I listed Mark in the credits as a co-director, along with my DP Justin McAleece who helped choose many of the shots and produce the film with me. Mark and Gina were kind enough to wait on payment for their work because we were friends.

My daughter had introduced me to Stephen after working with him at what I consider the best restaurant in LA, Gjilina after my former lead basically stole money from me for not doing his job. Despite it being his first film, I went with my intuition regarding Stephen. I was planning to cast him as the brother and not the lead, but then I cast Brian Goss as the brother and Stephen in the lead. Brian is now my writing partner on the Big Pharma corruption script *Tainted*.

Gina had already seen me produce *My Reality* in Malibu alone because I had flown her in for rehearsals. She had seen the insanity of me booking all the flights, locations, casting—basically every aspect of the film—without an assistant, which I desperately needed but had no money to pay for. My daughter visiting from NYC became my ad hoc assistant over the holidays, which truly was a gift from God. Not only was she so smart she had an internship with Vice News, but she was a graduate of University of Southern California journalism school where she had produced a weekly news show. Even after a great offer from a Vice producer (accused later of sexual harassment), she decided to go into mental illness nonprofit work.

During the rehearsals in November 2015, Gina helped with production booklets and other tasks, but her primary priorities had to be getting the role of "Clare" down and taking care of her son. I totally understood, and was particularly grateful for her husband's help with rehearsals and script revision, along with my daughter's assistance.

In order to keep going, I would often open a bottle of wine—when filming in Hawaii, it was mai tais—because the wine would give me another seven hours of energy. Worked every time! Of course, the mornings were never fun. I could cure my hangover fog with a workout, but if there was no time, I'd make a cup of coffee, take a hot bath or cold shower, walk the dogs, try to do a quick meditation, and be back at it by 8 or 8:30 am and go until 5 pm, then a remote meditation with Gary, or a nap, then open the wine at 8 or 9 pm and go until 2 am. All the same, October, November, and into December simply wasn't enough time to do the entire film myself. I had planned to start in August 2015, but then my daughter had gotten gravely ill in Istanbul. From Istanbul, we'd traveled to Italy, then New York City, until finally I was able to go to

Thailand for casting at the beginning of September, my original plan having been the end of July.

Later in September, I did the location scouting, then flew back home to Malibu to do preproduction and casting, then back to Thailand in November for casting and a quick 10-day trip to Burma (Myanmar) with friends when I thought I had enough money and should take a short break after working daily for five months (no one does a film in a year). Later, I realized that the film would cost so much more. Then just as I thought my head was above water, we had to change the lead to Stephen McClintic, because the former lead stole $8,000 and incurred $2,500 tickets on my car on New Year's Eve.

When Gina arrived in LA for New Year's Eve and Day rehearsals before we all left for Thailand to shoot *Bardo Blues* one month later, I'm sure she saw how overwhelmed I was. One woman can do a film alone, but at the risk of tremendous stress on body and soul. So as Gina observed everything I was doing, I left LA for Hawaii so I could stop drinking and try to look like a movie star while rehearsing lines over and over with my lead Stephen who had flown in. But I lost it when in Hawaii I received Gina's email asking about laundry facilities at the Thai hotel.

*How can you ask me this?* I emailed back.

She insisted my emails hadn't been clear. I'm sure she was right, given that I was doing the jobs of five people and had no assistant. The point was that I had no way of finding out about laundry except by yet another email to the line producer in Thailand or looking up the hotel and calling myself. Why couldn't she do that? Maybe she felt she'd helped me enough by accepting delayed payment, even though I was flying her son in because they had no one to help with him at home, plus I'd gotten them a hotel and an elephant tour. But she seemed to equate her own stress level over studying "Clare's" lines and mothering a child who didn't like to study with my level of stress.

Gina email: *Why is asking about what to do with my dirty clothes such a big deal?*

My email response: *Pack more clothing if you can't figure out if there is a laundromat nearby since the hotel room is only $25 and it's unlikely there will be a washer or drier since most Thai people clean their clothing in their sinks and hang them out to air dry.*

Immediately after our email volley, my body fell apart. I was due to be directing and on camera acting in three weeks; there was no room for illness. I basically emailed Gina that I was overwhelmed and could not cope with trivial questions I couldn't easily answer. I then flew economy to Japan, sick as a dog, to see my healer and then on to Thailand where I finally got better. All the while, listening to Chris Stapleton's song "Parachute" helped immensely to calm me and make me believe I could do this film.

Most of the filming in Thailand was truly heaven on earth. I know I am meant to make movies for the rest of my life because of all the joy it brings me. But it was strange that the only person who wasn't joyful on the set was my closest friend, and stranger still that I'd lost my other best friend while filming the previous film. I paid everyone equally, though it wasn't a lot of money, and felt that everyone was doing the film to support me and to have the experience of filming in Thailand, including Gina and Mark. I was so grateful to my team for being so positive, working hard, never once talking about the low pay.

Gina didn't show up until six days into the filming because she couldn't take her son out of school too much. When she arrived, Mark was on the set as Stephen's acting coach and co-director when I was in the scene. I noticed how tense Mark was after Gina arrived. I'd been friends with them for years and assumed Gina's tension was jet lag coupled with the dark role she had to play while caring for her son. But it wasn't jet lag: Each morning when we started our long days,

Gina was always somewhere between intense and tense. But I had way too much on my plate to deal with her anxieties.

The mood among the crew when Gina got there was one of palpable joy mixed with intensity because we had so much to achieve in a single day, given that there were no extra days (much less money) if we didn't nail the scenes. My cinematographer Justin was so ill he couldn't get out of bed and even had to go to the hospital after the 18-hour day before when he and his brother had had to film the chase scenes until 3 am when no one was on the road.

Then we filmed in Chiang Mai, arriving on a Thursday. We had permits for all the Chiang Mai scenes, but because more permits would have been prohibitively expensive, we snuck in a lot of people shots, including Stephen in the tuck-tuck, and then on Friday risked shooting the last scene of the movie at the very cool bridge. I was focused on directing and doing props.

Why was I of all people doing props? Picture not having enough money and yet having a killer hardworking team committed to your vision and working long hours, but you are still forced to do props while directing and acting, and the only reason you're doing the props in your scene is because it needs the coffee perfectly filled and you don't have the money to hire a prop or makeup person in Thailand, and the only other person on the crew who claimed to have tons of experience on movie sets was smoking cigarettes and taking behind-the-scenes photos.

After six days in a row, my scene was finally done and I was able to focus on directing Gina as "Clare," the owner of the whorehouse. By the grace of God, I had Justin's brother Ian as co-cinematographer; otherwise, we would have been in real trouble, as my DP Justin was now lying sick as a dog on the couch in the whorehouse in case Ian had to ask him questions. Yes, a real whorehouse with real clients walking by and picking out women. The owner said the only way we could work there was if they could continue to use the second floor for clients. It really fucked with our heads. Fortunately, none of the prostitutes in this tiny town in northern Thailand looked underage; in fact, as strange as it sounds, they all looked pretty happy. Not that I'm defending brothels, but this one wasn't at all as sordid as the Patpong "entertainment district" in Bangkok's Bang Rak.

My DP Justin made *Bardo Blues* possible in every way, including having a brother like Ian, an amazing cinematographer in his own right who was not afraid to admit while we were shooting the Buddhist cave scene earlier that day, "I need my brother behind the camera." In the earlier cave shots, Justin was bed-bound but now and then on set so Ian could at least ask him questions. I always shoot with two cameras, one on a tripod and the hand-held camera that Ian held.

I began directing Gina who had had many rehearsals in my home with Mark as her acting coach. We say Action! but she isn't good. She's awful. Perhaps she's rusty or just nervous. Great acting is all about knowing your role and lines and then relaxing. We did another take and she still wasn't good. Mark jumped in to direct her. He is the acting coach and I am the director on set; he is taking over my job without asking me. I am quiet.

Another take and no good.

This started affecting the other actors. My lead Stephen said nothing; we both had heard horror stories of sometimes as many as 20 takes, in contrast to Clint Eastwood's three takes. We got every scene in three takes except that night in the whorehouse with Gina. The issue was we didn't have the time or money for more takes; we had to nail every scene in three takes. If we had to have five takes, we would, but . . .

This can't be happening, I thought, and went in to give Gina direction.

Mark stepped in to try to help, which confused Gina, who said, "I don't know who to listen to."

How was I to answer? Tell your fucking husband who has been helping a lot up to this point to shut up.

Instead, I said, "Let's do another take."

She still didn't get it. I sat down with myself in the whorehouse filled with lady boys/transgenders. No one in Thailand can play a whore in a movie because it's disrespectful, but real whores surround my sick DP and best friend who can't relax or remember her lines enough to act. I am thinking, *The movie is over. I can't come back and re-film because the IRS is after me and no one will give me a loan because Hollywood considers me a failure because not one of my projects has sold since my 14-week failed late night show, so why not pack it up and go home? This cannot be happening to me. If my "Clare" lead can't do her part, the movie is over.*

So we just went on to the next scene. Mark kept interrupting me to direct his wife, and she kept doing a poor job, but I could tell we were getting something. I told my mind to stop thinking the movie was over. It was the most unbelievable mind game I had ever had to play with myself; next to my daughter dying, this was the most powerful mind situation I had ever been in. The two situations were the same test. Even if Gina didn't intend to ruin it, she was ruining it, so I had to believe nothing was going to get in my way of doing this film. Things could go dark and end, and if you don't truly believe in the light and that everything will work out, it won't.

After a very late night at the whorehouse, I went to bed. At about 2 am, I decided to have a look at the footage to see what was working and what wasn't. My editor Jason Shamai also viewed the footage and agreed it wasn't good. I couldn't cut out her role because the villain was 1/3 of the movie. What could I do? I invited Mark and Gina in before we were to due on the set and they watched. They didn't think it was that bad. I responded that I could not film the next scene at the computer store because I had to edit this to make sure it would work.

Mark and Ian (Justin was still in bed) left to shoot the next scene that I wanted to be at, but couldn't, because I had to salvage my movie. I couldn't tell Gina because it would just make her more nervous, so we did the rest of the scenes that night and they went better at moments, if not stellar. I knew she could be a great actress, so I relaxed and reminded myself that the fat lady hadn't sung yet. But I still didn't have the good-enough scenes from the previous five-takes night.

I talked to the line producer. We had scheduled one extra day for production just in case something went wrong. She talked to the Madam to see if we could film the next day and she said yes. We were the talk of the small town and she was losing business, but we put her in the movie with our actors—talk about Strasberg real life method!—and showed up for one more night of shooting.

Jason Shamai had spent all his time editing that one scene. Flying him over so I could make sure everything was working was the greatest move I ever did. We re-filmed the opening scene. It was never perfect, but it was good enough. (We edited most of it down so we wouldn't have to use it in the movie.) Then we did a few more retakes and everything was good.

Gina left town two days later with her son and sent me a bill for the extra day. I confronted her about charging me for her errors, and she reminded me of the big favor she did in coming at all and told me in the most poisonous email I have ever received how stressful the set was. Everyone else had the opposite experience and loved filming in Thailand; a few like Reggie the grip said it changed his life.

I paid Gina, having learned enough from Thich Nhat Hanh, the Buddhist monk who survived the Vietnam war, to not react but move on. I used to emotionally react to everything, but as the Beatles sang, Love is all you need. But I couldn't shake being in shock that my good friend would do this. Even waiting for her paychecks for a few months would have helped me.

When Graham committed suicide in 2016, I called her and Mark and we had a loving conversation for the first time since before Thailand. Graham had loved Gina, even had a crush on her for years. I wished her a happy birthday in July, and she wished me a happy birthday in December. In March, exactly one year after Thailand, I sent her the poison pen email and asked if she still stood by her perceptions on set. She said yes and wouldn't back down. There was nothing more to say. I moved on. No more happy birthdays.

Insisting that the actress is as important as the director / producer, even if the entire movie pays the price, iss beyond selfish. We had a difficult time editing her scenes to make them work, despite some of her stellar moments, but were happy that her performance merited awards. I extended the olive branch when the possibility of a special screening in Nashville came up, but she and Mark were too busy for it. They both contributed to the success of the film tremendously, and I will never speak to them again.

Loss of relationship may be part of the price of making movies and remaining loyal to one's vision through crisis. Had I continued to fear that the movie was over, it would have been over because I wouldn't have gotten the performance I needed. I reclaimed my calm center, worked with Gina's talented husband, and when Gina finally relaxed, we got the movie I had dreamed of, despite the loss of friendship.

But everything works out in the end, doesn't it? Graham stuck with me and my dream, even beyond death. My only regret is that he didn't see the finished movie. He would call and ask, "When is the screening?" Waiting to see the movie may have kept him alive longer, but when I pushed it back a few more months, I remember him asking, "Why?" He had no idea that we were filming the suicide scene during the 24 hours he was deciding he couldn't live anymore—or did some part of him know? I couldn't edit the suicide scene with Jason, so he did it. But I have had to watch it hundreds of times to sign off on the movie before we locked it, and hundreds of more times for festivals and private screenings. It's still not easy. My only solace is seeing his art and photo at the end.

Many times since his death, I've had the sensation of someone brushing against my shoulder. My stepsister Jenny had the same experience while editing her novel that she had hoped Graham would read. He has confirmed many times that this movie is true, and given me sign after sign that we continue living after death, but in a different form. I've felt a strange sense of peace for days, even in my awful grief. The day after he died, I heard him say *I am alive* through Eddie Vedder's voice in the song "Alive" by Pearl Jam, a song about how Eddie's father died before he knew he was his father and not his uncle, and that his stepfather wasn't his father. Every time I hear this song, I think how hard it must have been for Eddie, who then created a great artistic song out of his pain. So because my brother didn't believe in life after death and "Alive" came on the radio 15 hours after I found out he was dead, I heard the song completely differently. Graham knew how much I loved Pearl Jam, and I swear it was his way of telling me he was alive and the movie I created was true.

Did Graham also secure Pearl Jam's "Life Wasted" rights for the climax of the film? Julie Sessing, who helped me with the impossible task of securing Thai songs for the film, said, "There is no way you'll be able to afford that song." So I didn't even try. But six months later while getting the rights to songs, I was running out of money and thought, *What the hell, why not ask if a friend will give me a loan since everyone knows how much I love Pearl Jam.* Julie called, thinking there was no way I would get the song for under $150,000, and I got it for $10,000. I swear Graham did something from the heavens. My best friend Lilli Rey gave me a loan and "Life Wasted" was in *Bardo Blues*.

# 8

# In Quest of Healers

*Lower ego: So everything continues to pass down to each generation if the original wound is not healed?*

*Higher self: Yes, and over time family wounds change form, even entrenching as physical illnesses like cancer or parasites. Each of us inherits a particular theme. Yours is powerlessness. If you still feel it at 56, it isn't healed.*

*Lower ego: But I've studied with spiritual masters, meditated up to three hours per day, and sometimes dedicated my entire life to healing my wounds.*

*Higher self: I know. And your daughter was your final test.*

*Lower ego: I've done everything for her and suddenly have become powerless again. She tells me what I have done wrong as a parent, and I tried to do everything right. Every parent makes mistakes but I know when I die I will have no guilt because I was there for everything in her life unlike my father. Why must I suffer more? I thought I was done with suffering.*

*Higher self: Your daughter has to heal her own wounds in her own time. Once you fully heal your powerlessness, you will be done.*

> *Lower ego: So no emotional reactions to triggers, stop racing around . . . Beyond meditation, yoga, exercise, contemplation, what do I do?*
> *Higher self: Exactly what you are doing.*

Growing up in the northern suburbs of Chicago in a mostly Jewish section until high school, I was considered by all my friends to be the token *goy*. My mother would say, "We can't afford another bar mitzvah gift!" When I was 12 and 13 years old, I attended at least 63 bar mitzvahs (for boys) and bat mitzvahs (for girls). Looking back, I am so glad I grew up in that progressive, intelligent northern suburb of Chicago loaded with smart people and lavish parties. My stepfather was in the film inspection business with access to huge film libraries, so he made sure I had special films to play for my best friends at my simple, fun birthday party sleepovers. No one had parties like mine. All the way through high school, it was hanging together on Friday nights in expectation of beautiful Spencer Tracy-Katharine Hepburn classics.

So at an early age, I was watching 35mm films in the basement. Films offered a different escape than TV. Films had a beginning, middle, and end, whereas for TV viewers it is the ongoing emotional "hook" of characters from week to week. I was called the "walking TV Guide" on our block in Glenview, where over 30 kids between the ages of two and 18 lived. If I wasn't watching TV or at school, I was outside playing games with the kids in the neighborhood. I favored shows that made me laugh, escape from the reality of family dysfunction being the premium. At 13, I and millions of others were watching *The Brady Bunch* (1969-1974) and *The Partridge Family* (1970-1974), all about families being a fun effort of all ages working peacefully together.

My parents didn't let me watch Dark Shadows (1966-1971) or scary movies, but a few traumatizing films remain imprinted, like the birthday party film *Ring of Bright Water* (1969) about a beautiful otter that in the end is killed. My stepfather apologized for his choice; he had read only great reviews and never watched the ending.

I was also watching scary films during Friday night sleepovers at my friend's house. (I still have an eye phobia today from a film in which binoculars poked out eyes.) Her parents allowed us to watch horror movies, then took us to church each Sunday. For me back then, church on Sundays and sleepover horrors were just more escape from being glued to the TV at home to avoid alcohol-driven emotional scenes, like hearing my stepbrother being beaten daily for reasons I will never understand. My stepfather was a very funny man who loved watching *The Tonight Show Starring Johnny Carson* (1962-1992), but at 6 foot 5 and 200 pounds, he was also a very scary man. Later in college, I would turn to alcohol myself (and pot) to escape depression. Everyone drank in college. Did that mean they were depressed, too? Why was most of America, the richest country in the world, trying so hard to escape depression?

From truly human and artistic Spencer Tracy-Katharine Hepburn or Sidney Poitier films to what passes for much of film today, some sort of disconnect happened during the Cold War. For example, I was shocked when my ex-husband allowed our 7-year-old daughter to watch *CSI* (2000-2015) and the movie *Training Day* (2001). It has become painfully obvious that Americans have lost sight of what they are taking in and what it is doing to them psychologically and spiritually.

As for church, my *goy* parents always went on Christmas and Easter. Otherwise, I went with my friend's family. I dressed up every Sunday for the youth service at the beautiful Glenview Community Church and began to experience some inner peace. Initially, my parents saw that I was picked up and dropped off, but then they started going and eventually became involved in raising money and volunteering. My stepfather was the head usher for years. It was a family affair on Sundays if it wasn't too much stress for my mother to get all us four kids in the car. Sometimes it was just me and my stepfather since no one else wanted to go.

But my parents were never like the evangelical Mormons they left me with when they went to Europe and I was 16. Daily, the Mormons tried to convert me, as if spirituality was more about the club you were in than experience. At the time, I wasn't doing drugs or alcohol and was a leader in our church youth group learning about no judgment, unconditional love, and loving our neighbor as ourselves.

I remember how honored I felt that I was chosen to play Gabriel, God's communicator angel, in the Christmas church pageant that people drove miles to experience, because the choir was so good and the Christmas story was told like a Broadway play. One of our choir's top singers was Eric Gilligan, who went on to become a top writer in Hollywood and producer of *Roseanne* (1988-1997). One degree of separation, not six, from Hollywood! I remember sitting next to Eric, a very funny man with a great voice, and him saying to me, "Marcia, I can't stay on key because you are so off-key." Even my father Bill told me at seven to stop singing in the car because my voice was so bad. It broke my heart, but I still sing in the car when I'm alone or when I'm doing a comedy skit.

I may have been the lucky girl in a cool high school group, cheerleader, president of my class, and a leader in my church youth group, but I was secretly deeply lonely.

At 13, I was invited to an unaffiliated free church camp called Christian Life. With four kids to be put through college, my parents wouldn't pay for camp, so I went to Christian Life because it was free and I could escape into Nature for a week. It was there that I realized there really is a Christ power outside of the self. Through my amazing youth minister Al Guilfoyle, I began to discover that I could pray to something that actually existed and could help bring peace to me. Later, after years of going spiritually inward and reading every spiritual book I could lay my hands on, I would know that we don't have to look outside ourselves for God, that we are all the sons and daughters of God. I would come to know this power more deeply, through my meditation teacher Gary Springfield, as Christ consciousness. In Elaine Pagel's 1989 book *The Gnostic Gospels*, I would discover the Gnostic way of thinking from *The Gospel of Thomas* found among the Nag Hammadi texts in Egypt in 1945. Our task was to become our best version of Christ.

Through God, we rest in Christ consciousness from the day we are born as His children; we just don't know it. Even if you don't believe in religion, the possibility of awakening to the necessity of *re-ligio*—binding back together what has been torn apart by first forgiving and loving yourself, so that you can at last manifest your most radiant being—is the real quest driving human incarnation. Today I believe in the Radiant Light Christ brought, but having studied so many religions, I would call myself spiritual instead of Christian.

My youth minister Al knew me only as the bubbly happy leader who sold the most fertilizer to raise money for the Bahamas youth trip to help build schools. When I privately shared with him how sad I was inside, the look on his face was one of deep concern. He really heard me. He didn't realize that I was suffering from depression, not sadness; those who have experienced depression know how different it is from natural sadness. Depression is a chemical plague so debilitating that it makes you feel you can't cope and don't want to live. But just Al talking and listening lifted the awful unpredictable feeling. Who knows what being able to confide in Al saved me from? After camp, he continued checking in with me twice a week and during Sunday service.

Church was my escape from home, as was every school activity I loved doing. By the time I could drive, I was rarely at home.

When I was 17, I visited my father for six weeks on my own for an independent high school final year project. At that point, Dad was a full-on atheist; only in the last five years of his life did he become a practicing Buddhist. During a car ride after I picked him up, I recall how dead silent he was for most of the drive until turning to me and saying he suffered from depression and that I should look into therapy because it might help me. At the time, all I could think was that he was willing to pay for therapy but not willing to spend real time with me.

Six months before his second divorce, he had perceived that my depression was like his.

I was cruel to my younger sister—one, because my mother favored me and I took her lead, and two, I felt such sadness, loneliness, and desperation regarding our father's inattention that I took out my pain and anger on her, the next victim down the line. To this day, she blames me for her childhood trauma and won't speak to me. But where were the adults who in their greater wisdom should have been there for us? Who thought it fine for a three-and-a-half-year-old to push my little sister in the grocery cart until it hit the wall and my sister had to have stitches? And yes, I vindictively broke one of her favorite glass teddy bears at eight years old, and at 17, at my father's house, I said some cruel things. Our parents set the tone that led to her and my trauma. I never learned how to control my anger, the kind of training observing parents should provide. I passed on to her the hurt and anger I felt.

My spiritual path began in high school when I realized (*real eyes!*) 100 percent that Something bigger than me had created me and that I could pray to It for assistance. I called it God, but you could just as well call it Mother Earth, Higher Self, spirit, divine, Christ, etc. Such knowledge is very different from being a "good Christian" and may even go through a phase of not believing in anything divine.

My first college pick had been Colorado University in Boulder, but my parents said they couldn't afford it and were afraid I'd party too much. I hadn't even partied in high school; all I wanted was the magical spiritual energies of skiing in the Rockies. I was devastated. Bill Kimpton had given his children a true gift: he'd taught us how to ski at every Christmas and

Easter school break at Lake Tahoe. Wine and weed have provided my spiritual outs, but skiing was my primary spiritual in until I was mature enough to develop the disciplines of meditation and yoga after my father's death.

My father could have paid for Boulder, but my parents didn't want his help, and the truth is, they wanted me closer to home. Both sets of parents felt that I should just be grateful that my education was being paid for, but as I sit here at 56 in Aspen, Colorado, having finally come home to the Rockies I have wanted to live among since I was 17, I realize that I knew at a young age that for my soul I needed to be near the Rockies as well as near New York City, Los Angeles, and San Francisco for the arts I love so much.

Indiana University was where I first encountered yoga and meditation. For exercise, I swam in the IU pool, but through an off-campus yoga studio connected to an ashram, I began to see how the physical and spiritual interconnect and how everything I had learned in church through prayer was embodied in the practice of yoga. The English teacher who had agreed to be my independent major sponsor was one of the heads of the ashram that owned the yoga studio and my favorite health food store. (I had abandoned my TV communications major because I couldn't get enough hands-on production experience and had instead designed my own major so I could start producing rock videos, or anything else, with a camera and an editing room.)

On my last day before graduation, my ashram-connected mentor and teacher convinced me to come to his lovely home and meditate with him and his wife in a small room. At the end of our mediation, he asked if I wanted to move to Boston with them and the ashram. He may have thought he was helping me, but I intuited that he had been recruiting me into his cult all along! Having read my sad journals as part of the independent study, he knew all about my loneliness. I felt so betrayed.

When my father died, I started learning to relieve my pain not with alcohol and drugs but with Gary Springfield's golden light meditation and *bikram* yoga. With monthly trust fund money, I felt so fortunate that my father's money would now allow me more experiences, more travel, and more ability to pursue self-inquiry (not necessarily therapy).

When I couldn't get hired for television, I decided to concentrate on studying world religions, beginning with Emanuel Swedenborg. The draw to Swedenborg may have been because he too was visited by spirits of the dead and believed that the voices of schizophrenia were actually voices of the dead. This would all become terribly meaningful to me, given that I first heard from my dead namesake grandmother in 1992, and my brother Graham was diagnosed with schizophrenia the following year.

I spent eight years studying Swedenborg at the Pacific School of Religion (PSR). Swedenborg taught that everything—and I mean everything—has a spiritual correspondence, beginning with the omnipresent radiance of Divinity corresponding to the Sun of our natural world. The Sun's heat is love and its light wisdom, all of which we need for our own enlightenment and ability to love. The entire plant world upon which we depend for our sustenance would expire without our star. Love and wisdom in the spiritual world, heat and light in our physical world. Correspondence, as Swedenborg uses the term, is about a real, dynamic, ongoing relationship between divine and human love, divine wisdom and human enlightenment.

Swedenborg profoundly changed my thinking. From him, I also learned of the internal church. We are here to experience LIFE, including ferreting out and healing the traumas that threaten to prevent us from further growth. We can be gifted with great looks and innate skills, but if we wish to radiate from our internal church, we will need to heal.

At the Swedenborg Church in San Francisco, I asked Reverend Jim Lawrence, dean of Swedenborg studies at PSR, who Swedenborg was and where in heaven had my father gone. His answer was to hand me Awaken From Death: An Inspiring Description of the Soul's Journey into Spiritual Realms Upon Bodily Death, written in the 18th century.

I had no paying job and had suffered from serious writer's block for over five years, basically since my late night show had been cancelled. Hollywood had decreed that at 40 I was washed up. I bought into their thinking and couldn't come up with one creative idea. It was painful to stare into space with a blank white page. Today, I can't keep up with the plethora of ideas I have for scripts I want to write for both film and TV.

When my daughter went on trips with her father, I either went off to Asia to study Eastern religions or audited Swedenborg classes at PSR. I wanted a master's degree but couldn't manage the 600 pages of reading a week and the many papers. I had been undiagnosed ADD most of my life and wasn't willing to chemically alter my body in order to read and write, so I audited for years, taking many of the classes over again, like the classes based on the texts *Heaven and Hell and Its Wonders and Hell: Drawn from Things Heard and Seen (1758)* and *True Christian Religion, Vols. 1 and 2* (1770). Swedenborg was impossible to understand on my own, but Rev. Jim was a profound teacher. Through him, I realized we reflect heaven or hell, and that even if we are going through hell, we have a choice to get to heaven.

With Andrew, my longest relationship after my divorce and someone my daughter adored, I traveled anytime I didn't have my daughter—to Amsterdam, Berlin, Istanbul, Iceland, Bali, and India—at first filming comedy segments and developing a TV series called *Star* in self-mockery of my pursuit of stardom. It involved a rock star in Iceland, then a porn star (never did it) for which I interviewed a real porn star called Sunset ($2,000 per hour) on a porn set and her boyfriend / handler / pimp Dennis Hoff, who later got a HBO TV series based around his Nevada brothel, The Moonlite Bunny Ranch.

The third segment was a horror movie set at my father's home in St. Helena with the acclaimed horror film director Mark Borchardt, subject of the Sundance award documentary *American Movie: The Making of Northwestern* (1999). Our clever 3-episode TV series didn't sell, so we made it into a short film and got it into the Santa Cruz Film Festival.

When I reverted to the old pattern of being back in bed and depressed because nothing sold, I decided to do a retreat with Gary Springfield and really learn to meditate. Up to the first retreat with Gary, my version of meditation had been to sit on my bed, look at Alcatraz in the Bay, and let my mind unwind, or I would go for a run to the Golden Gate Bridge, daily exercise having proven to be the quickest way to chemically change my body and lift depression. My brother, like my father, rarely missed daily exercise. But when I went to Gary's retreat with Kristen in Sedona, he had something different in mind for meditation. As his voice takes you out to the Void, the golden light of your soul fills up your mind so that it stops thinking.

Now, 17 years later, it's rare that I miss my daily, if not twice-daily, meditation. I also meditate to the Dalai Lama's healing chant and am now able to silence inner thoughts so much so that if an idea rolls in, I just let it go and out it rolls, like the tide. Living in the present moment allows you to live in your intuition and Higher Self, which means streaming divine love instead of mind or ego. This has taken years of practice, but I love my life so much more now that I know how to live this way.

A few days ago I forgot to check my gas tank while driving in the mountains after a great show with the legendary bluesman Buddy Guy. Either my angel or Higher Self asked, *How much gas do you have?* I checked: six miles worth, and it was 15 miles home. With just a little bit of champagne, I could hear this voice direct me, like tuning into a fine radio station. I credit years of meditation for having proved to my Higher Self that I really am interested in its guidance. The Higher Self, guiding voices of angels and the dead all help us as we stumble along this lonesome Earth Bardo . . . If I hear the anger or fear frequency, it's the lower ego, and I move to just shut it off like a tap.

Meditation has also helped me to love the little wounded girl still wandering around somewhere inside. Besides Gary, I also credit Helene, whose surname I've forgotten. Both taught me to practice going in to find that wounded child whose memories deep in my cells and gut may still broadcast all around me as my life plays out her vibrational patterns over and over.

Did I think it would take until my 57$^{th}$ year to have my dream film distributed? No. I thought by healing myself daily, my dreams were right around the corner. Neither the 3-episode TV series *Star* nor my first movie *My Reality*—written, produced, directed, and acted in 12 days in San Francisco and 2 days of filming on the plains of Mongolia—has yet been seen by anyone, and neither got into a film festival. If you don't have a power agent, forget getting into Sundance.

When I wanted to film *My Reality*, I went looking for a cameraman and found Justin McAleece on a random website for red cameras. Justin became my partner in every project as a director of photography, producer and editor (until I met my current editor Jason Shamai), all the way forward to the award-winning *Bardo Blues*. Between *My Reality* and *Bardo Blues*, Justin also shot my first TV pilot *Planet M*, then two web series called *Planet M*, none of which sold.

So I kept meditating, clearing the vibrational patterns I was holding from childhood, by reflecting, contemplating, journaling, and practicing yoga. Thirty-five years after starting in the entertainment business, 45 years after having the vision of my own show, and 18 years after my father's passing, my dreams are clearing and coming true. Was it the meditations in Bhutan, Laos, Thailand, Cambodia, India, Rome, Greece, France, Kenya, South Africa, Botswana, Ghana, and 44 other countries I have visited that have finally given me the ability to clear the darkness and sadness from my soul, spirit, and vibrational field around my body to allow my dream to finally happen, or has it just been working hard year after year and not giving up? It has been both, not either-or. (Why do Westerners insist on locking everything into duality?)

About four years after my father passed, I read in the *New York Times* about the movie *Travelers and Magicians* directed by the lama Khyentse Norbu (Dzongsar Khyentse Rinpoche) of the tiny kingdom of Bhutan, which borders China and India. (Unlike Tibet, Bhutan has thus far been able to retain its sovereignty.) I had just started to really study Buddhism, and since I couldn't get work, booked a 3-day trip to Bhutan. Visitors were required to pay $200 per day to the royal family, the thinking being to keep the tiny kingdom pristine for "gross national happiness." (They had had TV only a few years.) Visitors were also required to pre-pay for a guide and hotel. Add it up and three days in Bhutan was around $3,000. Initially, I added Thailand and Vietnam, but after Bhutan's magic I couldn't get myself on a plane to Vietnam where I knew the magic would be immediately expelled by the documented horror of the Vietnam war. (I did eventually visit Vietnam and was deeply moved by all the tourist outlets selling the art of adults and children affected by Agent Orange.)

So I boarded a jet in Bangkok to Bhutan. While waiting two hours in the plane in Calcutta to pick up passengers, I underwent a full-on panic attack. I used to have chronic anxiety before daily meditation, so this panic attack was unusual. I kept thinking, I am getting off this plane and not flying into the Himalayas, I can't do it. But I had had to pay in advance and didn't want to forfeit $3,000 and miss this magical trip, so I went to the bathroom and talked myself through the attack, the sweat pouring down my face, my heart beating so fast I thought I was going to have a heart attack.

After ten minutes, I left the bathroom and scanned the passengers: All were white tourists, except for a handsome Bhutanese. I went up to him and said, "I am really scared to take this flight and am thinking of getting off. Can you please tell me if I am going to be OK?"

He responded immediately with confidence. "I know the pilots and have flown many times this route. You'll be OK. Here's my card. If you need anything in Bhutan, don't hesitate to ask."

I thanked him and went back to my seat. The doors closed, the jet took off, and the pilot announced, "The clouds have now parted so we can land safely in this weather."

In America, we land in all kinds of weather. My thoughts returned to fear. What if the weather changed in the next two hours? Bhutan had stunning architecture and traditional dress dating back to BCE, but how dependable were their jets, etc. Even today, landings in Bhutan are considered among the most dangerous in the world. I opened my book to distract my mind. All of a sudden, the handsome Bhutanese man was standing over me.

"How are you?"

I say I am OK, although I'm not.

"What book are you reading?"

I look at the cover. Beyond the Sky and the Earth: A Journey into Bhutan.

"Look at my card I gave you," he says, "then at the first page of the book to see who it is dedicated to."

Tshewang Dendup. What are the odds that I am reading the romantic story written by Tshewang Dendup's ex-wife about her experience as a Canadian English teacher in Bhutan and how she fell in love and had a child with him? A friend had recommended the book to me.

Tshewang Dendup's handsome face also looked vaguely familiar. "Are you the lead actor in Travelers and Musicians?" I had seen the film the month before. It was why I was visiting Bhutan.

He smiled, said nothing, and headed back to his seat.

We fly in on the scariest descent I have ever experienced. No, they don't have flight control; it is all done visually, which was why we had waited so long in Calcutta.

We land and I am on the tarmac of the most magical place ever. The beauty, the serenity, the peace is like nothing I had ever felt. I go to claim my bag and Tshewang comes up to me. "Call me," he says.

My paid-for guide sees me talking to Tshewang and informs me that next to the royal family, he is the most famous man in Bhutan. He was not only in Travelers and Musicians but was Bhutan's one and only news anchor for years. Tshewang grew up in a small Bhutanese village, then earned a telecommunications scholarship to UC Berkeley. When he graduated, he returned to his country to set up its first TV news station in 1992. He too was studying Buddhism and meditation under the Rinpoche film director who before Travelers and Musicians had done the award-winning film The Cup. Tshewang eventually gave up the news business in order to have less stress in his life. He helps the Rinpoche's foundation provide for the kingdom, but specifically concentrates on art and English programs for kids.

From my hotel room I called the most famous person in Bhutan and arranged to meet the next day after my return from the Tiger's Nest, the world-famous temple in Bhutan.

My guide then led me through local temples. I love Buddhism and wanted to meditate everywhere while observing the culture, dress and architecture. The Bhutanese are beautiful inside and out, the country transcendent and reflective of what Buddhism is supposed to be about.

In the morning I woke early and had a delicious Bhutanese meal of rice, beans and vegetables so I would have the strength to make the trek to the Tiger's Nest, which is built into the side of a mountain wall. Horses awaited us, but after 30 minutes of riding up the steep mountain, I dismounted and walked because the suffering of the horses was distracting me from the magical hike to the temple where every lama for thousands of years had meditated. I was exhausted when we arrived, but exhilarated. We'd started at 7,000 feet a few hours before and were now at 10,000 feet. All I wanted was to enter the temple and meditate.

Visitors can enter the museum but not necessarily the temple. I asked my guide if I might enter the private temple. He said it was rarely allowed unless one was a student of Buddhism and had planned ahead with the guide. I had assumed it would be like the temples in the valley of the day before and so asked him nicely again. When he explained to his friend the temple security man, the door opened. I will never forget entering the small meditation room where the XIVth Dalai Lama has mediated, along with multitudes of other holy ones across the ages.

I sat down to absorb the peaceful transcendent energy left behind by so many masters. I had felt this the first time I entered St. Peter's Basilica in Rome at 21, and again in Giotto's Scrovegni Chapel in Padua when I was contemplating suicide. This energy had saved my life. I had felt it years later in Patmos, Greece, considered the second Jerusalem by many, because St. John the Evangelist had been exiled there and had supposedly transformed the energy of the island into a magical oasis. I had felt it in Notre-Dame Cathedral in Paris, then again in a small church in NYC where I went every day to pray that I would stop smoking pot forever. It worked. And I have had this feeling during my retreats with Gary Springfield. Temples of the spirit move around! Most recently, I've found Todd Weldon. Walking into his home, I feel the divine temple.

I also felt this energy during a Natural World safari on the wide expansive plains of the Serengeti, but it wasn't as *contained* as it was in Tiger's Nest, where so many had meditated over the ages. By contrast, consider the spiritual darkness of the slaves of the Cape Coast Castle in Ghana enchained in one room. I never visited Auschwitz because I had too many Jewish friends and felt I would fall apart, but when I entered that Cape Coast Castle room, I could feel all the terror and darkness felt by the people who had been chained to the wall to be sold as slaves. Whether enlightened or victimized, sad or happy, one's spirit or soul parts remain in an energetic form in space. Horrific crimes against us, or those we commit against others, remain energetically until we heal our karma and become a Tiger's Nest temple ourselves. As Swedenborg taught, we are the church or temple and reflect our choices in our bodies, spirits and minds, so even if we don't know the details of our past karma, I believe we will eventually be brought by life experience to alchemize it into love. Feeling the suffering and love in all the temples and churches profoundly changed me and even saved my life. Call it God, Higher Self, Jesus Christ, Buddha, Divine Mother, Gaia, whatever you wish, but when I entered the Tiger's Nest there was no question that there was and is a Higher Power, and it is our choice as humans to access the heavens instead of the hells.

If you believe like I do that we are not just slabs of meat but eternal spirits that live beyond death (the point to *Bardo Blues*), you might also want to consider that you might as well figure things out now and not wait until you're dead or incarnating again. The fact that my brother didn't know what the story was but died on the day I was filming the *Bardo Blues* suicide scene with a lead actor who looks exactly like him points to the possibility that in the moments of transition from one frequency to another, he went from wanting to end his suffering to sharing my consciousness frequency through my film's frequency. He told me loud and clear through Eddie Vedder's Pearl Jam song "Alive" what a gift it is to be ALIVE!

One lesson from Bhutan stands out. When ten of us were sitting in meditation in the special meditation room of the Tiger's Nest temple, the woman next to me interrupts my meditation to say, "You're doing it wrong. You have to do your prostration first (kneeling before Buddha before meditating)."

I think to myself, What the hell, lady, I'm meditating. "I'm not Buddhist," I whisper back.

She stares at me. "Then why are you here?"

"To meditate," I say, then try to return to my meditative state.

Initially, I felt anger toward her, but then compassion and non-judgment overrode the anger. She may have studied Buddhism as a nice, white, wealthy girl with the means to get to Tiger's Nest, but consciousness isn't about protocols or doing it right. It's about feeling it, reflecting it, and being it. The only reason I'd been allowed to enter the temple was because I'd been honest about my study of Buddhism and attempt to reflect it in life, not because I was a card-carrying Buddhist. I try to never forget non-judgment, but my lower ego wants to judge people all the time. We mustn't judge because we don't really know what the other has been through in this life or others.

Before leaving Bhutan, I had lunch with Tshewang, and our chemistry was so amazing that we met later in Paris for an eight-day beautiful love affair and have remained friends ever since.

In Patmos, Greece, I meditated with Gary in the temple of the outdoors three hours a day three times a day for six weeks. There, I learned that if I meditated long enough, I could let go of all the sadness, grief, abandonment or anything I held in the vibratory field that no one could see but I could feel. Most people don't have the time or money to do such deep cleansing meditation because they are working for survival, but Gary said everyone has access to God's love, so even if they just stop for 20 minutes in the morning and 20 minutes in the afternoon, their entire life would change.

Meditation offers the perspective on how we are all creating and witnessing our movie on the screen of life with the ability to edit out any scene of past pain so we are no longer victims but victors. But it takes tremendous discipline, not through power yoga but through the yoga that clears one's field and the meditation that transmutes darkness into light. Patanjali said that yoga is the neutralization of the vortices of feeling. This is correct. Over these 17 years of working with Gary, I have seen tremendous changes in myself and him, including his great skill at beaming light into others from a distance.

*To be continued after the release of* Bardo Blues...

# 9

## Full Circle: Bill Kimpton on Escaping the Bardo

*Bhikkhus [monks], all is burning. And what is the all that is burning? Bhikkus, the eye is burning, visible forms are burning, visual consciousness is burning, visual impression is burning, also whatever sensation, pleasant or painful or neither painful nor pleasant, arises on account of olfactory impression, that too is burning. Burning with what? Burning with the fire of lust . . . The body is burning, tangible things are burning, tactile consciousness is burning, tactile impression is burning . . . The mind is burning, mental objects (ideas, etc.) are burning, mental consciousness is burning, mental impression is burning . . . Burning with what? Burning with the fire of lust, with the fire of hate, with the fire of delusion; I say it is burning with birth, aging and death, with sorrows, with lamentations, with pains, with griefs, with despairs . . . Being dispassionate, the Bhikkhu becomes detached; through detachment he is liberated. When liberated, there is knowledge that he is liberated. And he knows: Birth is exhausted, the holy life has been lived, what has to be done is done, there is no more left to be done on this account.*

*- The Buddhist Fire Sermon*

I heard from my father Bill Kimpton six weeks after he had died of leukemia. I knew it was him because I recognized his voice in my head. I was fanning the sheets over my bed one morning when I heard him say, "Heaven is far away and a glorious place where you keep on learning."

Before hearing from him, the very first dead person I ever heard from was my father's mother, my namesake grandmother Marcia. I had just picked up the peacemaker margarita my husband used for making up after nasty arguments and calling me a piece of shit, when I heard my grandmother say loud and clear, "Don't end up like me." She had had three very unhappy marriages.

In fact, I hear from the dead more often than I would like, and not just from relatives but from random people like my daughter's soccer friend's mother Linda, whom I knew only slightly, except that we both had lived through hellish divorces and custody battles. She popped into my head at breakfast one morning to say, "Our ex-husbands are the same, and look what happened to me." Both Linda and my grandmother died by alcohol and fire. I interpreted their post-mortem visits to be, at the very least, warnings about depression and alcohol.

Marcia Drennon Kimpton, my paternal namesake grandmother, had been a part of Chicago high society greatly because her third husband Lawrence A. Kimpton (1910-1973) was chancellor of the University of Chicago. When they married, Lawrence Kimpton was administrative head of the Manhattan Project; he was also a director of Standard Oil of Indiana. Newspaper clippings described my grandmother as a dynamic, beautiful woman who raised millions for the University of Chicago. In the late 40's and early 50's, fundraising was about all high-society women were allowed to do. At 18, she gave birth to my father and left him for her parents to raise—his father having left when he was born—while she went off to college and traveled internationally. I was one when she died at 48 after having drunk a little too much wine while talking on the phone to a friend and dropping a lit cigarette on her polyester nightgown. She burned to death for three days. I still can't take hot baths or light a fire in a fireplace without thinking of her.

So what do you think? Two dead women pay me a visit to warn me about the treacherous triangle of men, marriage, and alcohol, and both women died by alcohol and fire—oh, and I shouldn't forget the time when I passed out on dextro and tequila and was awakened (and saved) by Frank, my friend Neka's father, who had just died and clearly said to me, "Wake up! You are dying."

Neka was the acupuncturist who helped me during the dark court evaluation that took my daughter away from me to an East Coast boarding school where the amazing Farmens at the Rumsey boarding school became her second parents (there is always a silver lining) and she won a top award two years later for community service and academics. Neka went on to develop Urban Remedy, the purest, highest vibrancy organic food I've ever had.

As per our family history and ancestral repetition of patterns, my father had abandoned me as he had been abandoned, and so I continued abandoning myself for years through depression and alcohol. As with my dad, others viewed my use of alcohol as moderate, but who was I kidding? Anything beyond two glasses is masking sadness and abandonment.

Unfortunately, my gift of hearing from the dead does not seem to include the people I'd really like to hear from, like my brother Graham, except right after he died when I heard from him in the Pearl Jam song "Alive." He continues to show many signs that he is here as my angel, but I only heard his voice once, the same as my father.

Emanuel Swedenborg heard from the dead day and night for 34 years. In a restaurant, he heard Christ advise him, "Don't eat too much."Now if I were going to hear from Christ, that wouldn't be what I would expect him to say, but as I do eat too much, I would thank him and ponder why in his greater wisdom he said what he did. Did Christ say that to stars who become anorexic because they misinterpret what he is really saying? I look thin because of my height, but I need to lose 15 pounds. I am now 40 pounds heavier than when I did my late night show, back when I was not eating so as to compete with Hollywood starlets. The truth is that if you eat too much, it lowers your vibration and you no longer have a clear channel to God. I struggle daily with this, praying for ease in my body. Man does not live by bread alone, and if I am brutally honest with myself, this aspect of myself indicates that I am not yet able to remain in heaven on Earth. I can't recall if I ate breakfast the morning I heard from my father or brother, but I can tell you I was thinner. Maybe there should be a diet book called *If You Want to Hear From the Dead, Stop Eating So Much.* (Hey, every other diet book exists, so why not?) Most mediums I've encountered are overweight. What's going on there?

Sondra Sneed, the healer who claims she hears from God and wrote *What To Do When You're Dead: A Former Atheist Interviews the Source of Infinite Being* in 2013, said I should be a medium because I hear from the dead. But I don't want to be a medium.

"Why not?" Sondra asked me.

"Because I don't like hearing from the dead. I like making movies."

"But if you don't follow your true gift, you will be off-course your entire life."

Thanks, Sondra. So am I veering off-course because the last profession I want to do is listen to dead people trying to contact their loved ones, or am I saving myself from veering off-course by not hanging out my psychic shingle? It's true that the dead have helped me with the deaths of both my father and brother, and I am truly thankful for this, but I have no desire to become a medium.

Her predictions to me were dead on (no pun intended). She said I should at least be talking about the dead in the media. Having forgotten her profound predictive readings, I wrote the story about living in Bardo that became *Bardo Blues*. When the film was completed, I realized how right she had been in that my message was to show the living what I believe happens when we are dead in Bardo and hopefully what we can do before we die to reconcile the darkness we all have to reconcile. So if Sondra said I was destined to be a messenger for the dead, I believe she was right.

Anyway, when I heard my brother's voice, I booked an appointment with psychic Dannion Brinkley who has died three times—heart attack, brain aneurism, struck by lightning and pronounced dead for 24 minutes until he moved in the body bag—and now communicates with people on the other side. During the two weeks I waited to see Dannion (busy helping war veterans transition and talking to people like me about their deceased loved ones), my brother's signs of still being alive proved more and more that the voice I'd heard was his in the song "Alive."

I'm here to tell you that it is true: we never really die.

I've felt hesitant about relaying truthful but dark memories, especially given that Bill Kimpton, founder of Kimpton Hotels and innovator of the boutique hotel industry, is iconic to many and admired by employees and friends alike who respected his generosity, kindness, humility, intelligence, and most of all his humor. Who was I to shovel dirt onto the head of a hotel icon? But on the other hand, if given enough polishing and refining, even rocks shine like precious stones. Besides, Bill Kimpton gave me his father's blessing in his mandate, Write what feels right so you can heal it for your ancestors, including me. I heard this loud and clear from the "other side."

So that's part of what this book tries to do.

Why beat around the bush? Bill Kimpton was a shitty father who had a shitty father and shitty stepfather, and I have

147

had to rise to the challenge of tragedy disguised as family life to force myself to come to terms with family stumbling blocks so I can own who I am. Such is how the karma of generational abandonment works in the sticky, webby Kimpton Bardo.

Before Dad had the vision for his company, the white-walled hotels across America were lonely, ugly, and served bad food. Over the 30 years he'd traveled the world for his investment banking job, he'd grown tired of awful American hotel rooms, whereas European hotels had style, comfort, and a certain personal touch when you checked in and someone stepped forward to welcome you. The rest is history. When he died at 65, America had 34 of his uniquely styled hotels with chefs like Masa and Wolfgang Puck, thus initiating the celebrity chef culture in hotels. When Kimpton Hotels was sold to Intercontinental Hotel Group in 2014 for $430 million, it had 62 hotels. Today, the brand is expanding around the world with another 40 hotels in the pipeline.

When I asked the trustees and my two sisters (who had a vote) why they sold Dad's legacy, the trustees' response was that next to the sale of the Four Seasons Hotels, the Kimpton Hotels sale was the highest hotel sale in the world because CEO Mike Depatie had done such a great job sustaining Dad's vision. It was, however, painful to watch how the original investors and founders got left behind, but does any company expand with total integrity? Maybe Kat Taylor's Beneficial Banks do, but it is rare. In the end the Kimpton Hotel investors, trustees, and family took money over risk and headaches. My voice was not listened to, even though I fought the sale.

Granted, I wanted to be a filmmaker and not build a hotel empire. Everything is corporate today, everything for the bottom-line, but I think that so far, IHG has done a pretty great job of holding onto Dad's vision. True, they always treat me great when I arrive because I'm a Kimpton, but the Dewitt Hotel in Amsterdam, their first IHG hotel expansion under the Kimpton brand, still includes the Dutch greeting and friendly smile just as Dad envisioned. Full circle: he was inspired by

European hotels, and now the Kimpton Hotels will soon be in every major European city. Keeping that personal touch with millions of employees is definitely the challenge. I pray that IGH never loses sight of Dad's hotel innovation that the customer is the most important—rare today in our busy corporate world.

Who knows? Maybe I was wrong to resist the sale. There are so many boutique hotels today, and it's so competitive, that you need a Mike Depatie to make other ventures possible. But how do you replace a charismatic Bill Kimpton? As the founder, he was irreplaceable, and for that alone I am grateful. I was his daughter, despite all the difficulties in being his daughter. A conundrum, for sure.

Beyond his obsessions with money, control, and manipulating people, Dad was incredibly engaging. His movie star good looks and charisma inspired people to say how much he looked like George Clooney, to which he would quip, "George looks like me." Dad's eyes were Paul Newman blue, and he even found a way to meet Paul Newman and convince him and Warren Beatty to invest in his hotels. I'll never forget when Dad boasted of being in the editing room with Warren while he edited *Reds* in 1981. *Reds* won 12 Academy awards.

Dad loved movies. Whenever I visited my father in San Francisco, we would watch a movie together. (I still wonder if he secretly wanted to be a movie star.) He'd modeled briefly in Chicago for extra cash, and one night was featured on Hugh Hefner's *Playboy After Dark*.

Dad was dynamic, captivating, and funny. Everywhere I went with him, I felt important just for being with him. People turned when he entered a room, and when he spoke, you could hear a pin drop, which for his daughter was exciting and painful, given that he rarely listened to me. My favorite moments were at Thanksgiving family dinners where he would tell hysterically funny stories, like when his good friend Wally took a woman's shoe off at a formal dinner table, poured wine into the shoe and drank it. As the rebel in the room, Dad loved

149

anyone who did crazy things in proper formal settings.

When he became successful, his free spirit shocked many. His rebel thinking inspired all of his children: Jenny's outside-the-box, brilliant Pulitzer Prize book; Laura's mind-blowing Burning Man art featured in many cities; my wacky comedies so edgy that they made my mother uncomfortable; Graham's art still breaking limits today. We are all artists.

I spent years looking for a handsome, funny, brilliant, entertaining, charismatic and generous clone of my father. When I did marry, I thought my husband embodied my father's good side but finally had to admit it had been my father's shadow or dark side that I'd been subconsciously drawn to. Through my father's struggles to awaken to his karmic burdens, his struggles became mine as I strove to reshape my life from victim to victor. Generational lessons are the name of the Bardo game on Earth. My father and mother were impacted by their parents, who were impacted by their parents, who . . . You get the picture.

At eight, Bill was sent by his mother to a boarding school where he was made to feel stupid for being an undiagnosed dyslexic. His second stepfather physically and emotionally abused him, going so far as to shout over and over that Bill would come to nothing, which Bill countered with a passionate vow that he would be materially successful and not a nothing—a vow he achieved but at the expense of two wives and four children. Dad was never physically abusive, but he did pass on the unconscious unresolved issues he had with his father, stepfather, and mother.

What if I told you that Bill Kimpton, as a formless, timeless part of the Universal Oneness, decided to return to square things with his daughter and offer her a few tips on how to get out of the generational Bardo and maybe even turn the Hollywood Bardo on its head? Would you believe me? His decision to finally give me some of his time (now eternal) was no doubt quickened by my stirring things up while writing my version of Neale Donald Walsh's *Conversations With God*

(1995) in hopes of liberating myself from the illusions life is loaded with (which must be why I love making movies, right?). Our Kimpton *My Dinner With Andre* (1981)—the character Wally Shawn's first line is "The life of a playwright is tough"—began with what I thought was my Higher Self commiserating, *Life is hard, Marcia*, to which I responded—

Marcia: Really hard.—Dad, is that you? All I ever wanted from you was a shoulder to lean on or a hug once in a while. I get that you had no hugs growing up, so how could you recognize that I needed them more than I needed advice and correction? How could I be blown away by what you'd achieved when all I wanted was a loving father?

Saint Bill: Marcia, I completely agree and am so very sorry for being inept as a father.

*When he says Marcia in that dad-like voice, I feel him and know he is really here. I take a deep breath. Wow. What an opportunity!*

Marcia: But you didn't fuck it all up, Dad. We had laughter and good times, too, and you were better than either your father or stepfathers. I concentrate on the tragic parts because talking them out makes me feel better. In the end, maybe all an adult child can ask for is a father who was a better father than his father was.

*It sounded right, but . . .*

Saint Bill: You'll see the perfect plan soon, Marcia, I promise.

Marcia: OK, I'm waiting patiently, but I don't want to see the perfect plan too soon, if it means I have to die to see it.

*He laughed, and I took another deep breath. Talking over the Great Divide to the dead takes a certain amount of courage, and energy.*

Marcia: And thanks for the money in the end, Dad. A lot of people just end up with nothing, nada, no money, no nothing. I feel awful admitting that I was relieved when you died, but it wasn't about the money. It was about the emotional trauma ending of waiting for you to love me. All I wanted my whole life was for you to love me, but you couldn't. You didn't know how. I actually didn't think I'd get a dime because you made sure to tell us kids we wouldn't get any money except for emergencies. I had no idea what your net worth was, nor did I care. You made it, you enjoyed it, and you were always so modest to the point of not even driving your used Mercedes. But those asshole trustees.—I know, Dad: I'm lucky to have them as a problem, but they wouldn't even pay for a breast reduction.

*He laughed again.*

Marcia: You think that's funny, huh? Two old white men sitting on millions decide I have to keep big sagging boobs deforming my back.

Saint Bill: But in the end, the insurance approved it.

Marcia: Well, if you saw that, then you saw everything that happened.

Saint Bill: I did.

Marcia: I sure wish I could see you and hug you right now.

*Dead silence.*

Marcia: And when Lawrence Kimpton, your second stepfather, basically said, 'Fuck you' by leaving you only one dollar and your mother's chairs, how did you recover?

Saint Bill: I put my focus on work and making my own money. I channeled all the darkness into making something good, but in the process left a trail of darkness for you and your sister, mother, and brother to deal with. And look what happened to Graham—mental illness. I tried hard to make it up to him, but it didn't work. Either he couldn't escape his karma or he was just too sensitive, or in my ignorance I couldn't see what I was really doing. Probably all three.

*Our sadness for Graham intermingled.*

Marcia: I remember Grandma dying when I was one and my feeling your pain and terror. My studies with different healers—specifically, Gary Springfield—helped me go back there and feel the tremendous grief. In their first six years, children pick up on everything in their family, so that the trauma keeps playing out vibrationally until it is made conscious and healed. Did you see that, Dad, when you passed to the other side?

Saint Bill: I did.

Marcia: So you built a mini-empire and had a stepfather who left you a dollar and a biological father who was a superstar basketball player who left and never looked back and whose career ended at 26 as an alcoholic on Skid Row, until 30 years later he shows up sober and asks you for money. You forgave both of them and let them see their grandchildren. Amazing how you can forgive, Dad. Do you think I'll ever get there?

Saint Bill: I do, Marcia.

Marcia: Father trauma shaped both of our lives, Dad. Parents war against their own children because their parents warred against them when they were children. It's a big, long, ugly karmic chain—

*At least I hadn't done that with my daughter.*

Marcia: Dad, from where you are now, how much of our life is pre-determined and how much is free will?

Saint Bill: It is both. Once we take responsibility for our lives and see how it can all lead to good in the end, we are in charge and in control of creating and shaping it. I just didn't know this until I died.

Marcia: This might be an opportune time, Dad, for me to recite my *Eight Negative Gratitudes*, to which you might choose to say I'm sorry for every one you recognize as true:

*Gratitude 1:* Thanks, Dad, for when I was three years old and you didn't have the money to pay the electric bill so the lights went off, thus imprinting me to not pay bills on time and not have savings, but like you, always believing that things would work out.

153

Saint Bill: *Mea culpa.*

*Gratitude 2:* Thanks, Dad, for abandoning me at three and a half.

Saint Bill: *Mea culpa.*

*Gratitude 3:* Thanks, Dad, for shocking my system when you picked me up at eight years old at my mother's house and took out a map to show me the state of California, explaining that you were moving to San Francisco without me.

Saint Bill: *Mea culpa.*

*Gratitude 4:* Thanks, Dad, for telling me at 12 years old when I got my period and the Kotex stopped up the toilet that I was a fuckup by screaming, 'Why the hell did you do that, Marcia?' Obviously, it hadn't occurred to you that no one told me you couldn't put Kotex down the toilet. But you did apologize. I can't remember many apologies, but I remember that one.

Saint Bill: *Mea culpa*, Marcia, I should have apologized more often.

*Gratitude 5:* Thanks, Dad, for not showing up to anything I did when I was a child and young adult, except one ballet recital.

Saint Bill: *Mea culpa.*

*Gratitude 6:* Thanks, Dad, for being too busy to pick up my phone calls and hardly having time for dinner, lunch or coffee when I moved to San Francisco and especially when I was so lonely after my divorce. Weren't you lonely after your divorce, Dad?

Saint Bill: *Mea culpa*. I stuffed it and just worked.

*Gratitude 7:* Thanks, Dad, for changing your will on my birthday three days before Christmas. Did you see the tears in my eyes when I heard your net worth was $130 million and yet you wouldn't give me a loan for my late night show?

Saint Bill: *Mea culpa*. No one gave me a loan.

*Gratitude 8:* Thanks for never considering that Hollywood might be harder for a woman. I'm trying hard here tonight as I write this and hear you, Dad, to not be a victim.

Saint Bill: *Mea culpa*, Marcia. I had no idea of how to be a parent of a son or a daughter, nor did I understand Hollywood beyond its allure.—But if you were over here, Marcia, you'd see how perfect it all works out . . .

Marcia: Depression, anger and sadness perfect? That's hard to accept, Dad. How can it be perfect?

Saint Bill: Marcia, once you get here, you will know that you are a piece of God. When we can remove our mother's and father's masks, we realize we are our own mother and father. In fact, we are God and must learn to love ourselves better and deeper than our father or mother ever could. Then we realize how perfectly the school of the Earth Bardo is karmically set up.

Marcia: It took me 15 years after you died to even begin to realize I was caught in a Bardo and begin studying how to figure out a way out of it.

Saint Bill (*shrugging*): It takes as long as it takes. Look how long it took me. Living is hard, Marcia, and we continue to learn after dying.

Marcia: But it has to be easier without a body—isn't it?

Saint Bill: You studied Swedenborg, so you know we don't really die. We just transition and set to work on all the same lessons in a different form. I saw when you woke up to knowing you never die.

Marcia: You saw when I was driving and had that scary moment when I realized that everything continues and there is no way of escaping it?

Saint Bill: Yes, and waking up to knowing you have to handle every situation and every heartache, every trauma that comes at you because inevitably you created it.

*I created it all? I contemplated the trajectory that could have preceded this life, the themes of abandonment, learned helplessness, and abuse of power that made me choose parents and men who would make sure I experienced powerlessness. Was it possible?*

Marcia: How the hell did I create these traumas? A child doesn't consciously choose terror and disappointment.

Saint Bill: No, but the force or energy of whatever happened in your last life on Earth leaves an energy footprint you must continue to work with.

Marcia: So I cut off the head of my ex-husband and he came back to ruin my life?

Saint Bill: No one comes back to 'ruin your life.' The energy sets your life up so you have to undertake everything that comes at you without resistance. I was as caught in it as you. And like me, you resisted most of what happened to you, and in your anger you drank like me. That we knew how to stop at three or four glasses meant we were in resistance and not total self-destruction. Acceptance of our fate so we could work with it instead of against it is what we needed. We both found meditation and yoga, and now you aren't fighting but are accepting your self-created destiny, as hard as that might be to accept. Now, you accept and observe what comes at you in 'neutral' because you know you were involved in creating it. The greatest teaching of both Buddha and Christ is unconditional love for ourselves, for others.

Marcia: But children of rape or violence . . .

Saint Bill: Marcia, no one consciously creates anything, but darkness pervades planet Earth along with the light. Each of us is on assignment to alchemize the darkness, based on what we have learned from past lives. Did that child as an adult in a former life rape someone and only see the big picture in their death? I don't know. It is important to realize that some people who did nothing to deserve their suffering come like angels to experience the darkness in the most brutal ways and thus learn to carry and transform it to help others without becoming its victim. No one knows another person's journey, nor can anyone sit as judge over another life—thus the lesson of compassion towards others and ourselves as we seek to learn the ultimate lesson.

Marcia: Which is what, Dad?

Saint Bill: That whatever you are given in your life, only you can choose to take responsibility for changing what needs to be changed. You must find the way to transmute the darkness thrown at you, and your process of transmutation helps your ancestral lineage, yourself, and your descendants. In this way, we all help humankind. We make the world a better place if we can shine real light.

*Bill Kimpton, my dad, really had become a saint of deep understanding. He went on:*

Saint Bill: The physical plane also has its own moments of joy, love and happiness mixed in with dark forces that are not personally 'yours.' The level of your emotional involvement indicates what is and is not your responsibility. Every time you are triggered, an emotional wound probably needs healing. Eckhart Tolle referred to it as the 'pain body.'

Marcia: But what would have become of me if you hadn't left me any money, Dad? Remember how you tallied all the money—including 20 years of 'gifts' and my ex-husband's divorce settlement—then told me I was a fuckup when it came to money? I can still feel my anger, Dad. Money obviously still triggers my unworthiness wound. Remember how after all your years of meditation and Spirit Rock silent retreats, you asked to meet me for a special walk to the Golden Gate Bridge. I was so excited! I was going to have time alone with my successful, busy father. Then you pulled out paper and added up every penny of your money I had spent since college, even presenting me with a bill for what you had said had been 'gifts.' And why the fuck did you add in the divorce agreement? My lawyer even made me sign a letter saying I wouldn't sue him when I realized I hadn't gotten nearly what was owed me from your darling ex-son-in-law, because I wanted us to get along for our child's sake—and he is still angry at me. I admit it, Dad: I'm not good with money. I thought I would make millions with my art. But with a failed marriage, a failed career, and a huge IRS tax lien, I have had to find a new way to validate myself and find love through God and meditation because the outer earthly Bardo values me exactly as you did: a failure. But I'm far from being a failure, Dad! I've never compromised my body or my integrity for the ruthless, spineless, sexist entertainment business, and have created art, despite very few having had the opportunity to see it.

Saint Bill: Marcia, your feeling of unworthiness comes from my having bequeathed to you the darkness I received from my parents when they abandoned me. You and your daughter—my granddaughter—are transforming our dark ancestral cycle. I couldn't be more proud of you.

*Tears filled my eyes at the mention of my daughter.*

*They say the sins of the father travel through the ancestral line unto the third generation (or until it is consciously healed). Years after my dad died, my 17-year-old daughter contracted a grave illness on a community service trip to Thailand I had signed her up for. The doctors couldn't find anything wrong; in fact, the head of the UCSF Infectious Disease Clinic went so far as to write a letter stating that my daughter and I had made up the entire illness, which no doubt influenced my ex-husband to interpret the illness as anorexia and take me back to court.*

*Needless to say, all of this served to keep me in the lower vibration of fear, hopelessness, and powerlessness (just like my childhood), and I know that my daughter was experiencing powerlessness with her father just as I had with mine. As her mother, I felt powerless to heal her and powerless in the court system that kept her from me and even dictated what doctors I was to take her to, namely doctors committed to a corrupt medical system that wants us sick and thus contributes to our powerlessness by not curing us since health doesn't make money. After 100 doctors, five emergency visits, and a multitude of hospital visits, I know how true this is.*

*She died briefly in my arms in Istanbul after a low-potassium seizure, the parasite that no doctors or labs had found having basically eaten her alive. I remember walking into the Turkish hotel room in Istanbul with the hotel manager and there was my daughter having a seizure on the floor. The manager raced to call 911 as I began mouth-to-mouth resuscitation. Death clamped my lip in her teeth as I watched the darkness spirit her beloved light away. (Walking through Istanbul the next day, my bottom lip was eight times its normal size.) I prayed to all the powers—Buddha, Jesus Christ, anyone and everyone—and she miraculously returned on my breath, the same breath that began her life in my womb.*

*The emergency responders did not speak English. My daughter kept taking her clothes on and off, and the three EMTs couldn't get her into the gurney, so I grabbed her, dragged her with the true goddess power of a mother to the elevator with the ER man helping, and finally delivered her to the ambulance. Never in my life have I seen such incompetence, though I must add that I love the Turkish people, especially the manager who literally saved my daughter's life.*

*The doctors in the ER unit spoke English but were arrogant and didn't care about my poor daughter. They basically did nothing but take her blood, then demand I pay in Turkish cash, not a credit card, for an MRI to see if there was brain damage. My daughter was out of her comatose state and in such fear that she didn't want me to leave her side. What was I to do? I left to look for the closest ATM at midnight, explaining that I hoped someone would attend to her. When I returned, she had had a shot I didn't approve. I was in shock. When I asked the doctor what had happened, he said she'd had another seizure, so they'd drugged her. They still didn't know that she was potassium deficient. Only by the grace of God did she not die of a heart attack.*

*The next day, they finally figured out the potassium deficiency and slowly infused potassium into her body. Two days later, we took a huge risk and continued our planned trip to Mykonos, Greece, it still being too risky to fly home while she was taking potassium tablets. Going to the beach was too difficult, she could hardly move from her bed to the pool, and loud noises made us return to the hotel room. A spiritual master told me that when one dies and then returns to the body, the spirit finds it painful to be back in the body.*

*At last we found a doctor who tested her blood on a regular basis, and ten days later he approved our flight back home. En route to Milan, her fingers started cramping and she couldn't breathe. EasyJets are not easy because you get what you pay for. We hooked her up to the one oxygen tank onboard and were informed that we would have to land in Florence, because there was no other air tank. If she utilized ¾ of the tank, the plane must land in case someone else needs oxygen.*

*At that moment, potassium loss was not the issue; potassium levels were fine, plus she was taking the tablets. So I made the scary decision to lower her oxygen intake without her knowledge because the drama of landing early could be worse.*

*Sure enough, the ambulance was waiting in Milan, and they wanted to first check her out. But just as in Istanbul, no one took us seriously, and I could only find one doctor who spoke English. When I told him she was potassium deficient, his eyes popped open and he immediately ordered blood work and a heart sonogram, and we were back with a potassium drip and couldn't fly home. Fortunately, I found a hotel with a resident doctor who for three weeks monitored her blood until she could safely travel to Zurich, Switzerland, where another top doctor did the same tests. I was so grateful that my father had provided enough money for any medical emergency.*

*Five weeks later, we made it home, but it took eight years to find the right doctor, tropical medicine specialist Kevin Cahill, MD, in New York City, who finally found the ringworm parasite from Thailand—just as I had told the doctors. Had I listened to the UCSF doctors, my daughter would have died.*

*Three times my ex-husband and I ended up in the court system labyrinth over custody of our daughter. When she finally turned 18, she went before a judge on her own and declared that she was changing her surname to Kimpton.*

Saint Bill: Remember, Marcia: You chose your mother and me as your parents, just as your daughter chose you and her father. Before we enter this earthly Bardo, we have our pick from among millions of parents. For whatever reason, you decided you wanted us and she decided she wanted you. That's what I've learned here.

*Parents weren't the luck of the draw? Wow.*

Saint Bill (*sad*): I tried hard with Graham, Marcia. I had abandoned you and your sister while amassing wealth, and I did my best to find fault with you because you were your mother's golden child. I was determined with my third child, my son, to give him all the attention I hadn't given you and hadn't gotten from my mother or father. But I ended up losing

161

him, too. Either he couldn't escape his karma or he was just too sensitive.

Marcia (*sad*): It was devastating, Dad, how you gauged Graham's and my paths as artists according to our monetary success. Why did you look down on art that doesn't make money? You viewed both of us as failures.

*The pain of having lost Graham pierced me anew.*

Saint Bill: Money was how I defined myself, so money was how I defined you. It doesn't mean anything where I am now. We grow up reflecting the vibrational patterns of what is around us, repeating them over and over until life hopefully brings us experiences to show us how to break out of those patterns. My stepfather conditioned me to be a failure, and it terrified me. I figured if I made a million dollars, I would be safe from being a failure. But after my first million, I became depressed. Money didn't make me happy! That's when I got into meditation. On Earth, money makes life easier because you don't have to think about survival, but no one should value himself or herself based on money. Money's a tool, an energy that can help or hinder one's quest as to why we return to the Earth Bardo again and again.

Marcia: And yet I thank you, Dad, for the money you left me, and for paying for my 20 years of therapy, though the most I got out of it was how talking about my problems helped to clear my head. But you added the therapy to the bill you presented me with—Holy shit! The resentment again.

Saint Bill: Peace takes many lifetimes, Marcia.

Marcia: But I want it in this lifetime, Dad. I should have bought a bat and hit a tree for an hour a week and spent the $80,000 you spent on my therapy on my film. But no regrets—that's how we learn, right, Dad? Now after 34 years of working in film, I'm finally getting awards. No money yet, but I've learned not to continue the thought pattern of money as the only sign of success. I choose instead to view success as a balancing act. I'm an artist as well as a kind and loving mother trying her hardest to find enlightenment, even if it is fucking hard and seems elusive and absurd in a world run by Bardos.

Now after your death, you're taking off your mask and allowing me to see how perfect you've been for my life's journey. I sought to blame others because I didn't realize how the Bardo and karma thing works. My dream of a happy family and being the queen of late night comedy has to fit with being a successful Marcia healing herself and her lineage. At 56, anything is possible, except maybe a second child.—That's a joke, Dad.

*I could feel my dad beaming at me.*

Saint Bill: I love you, Marcia. Again, I'm sorry I valued money and wanted you to buy into my values, no pun intended.

*Saint Bill is swimming among my dark ancestral cells sustaining a soul disease desperately in need of the light of consciousness and self-forgiveness. He'd walked out when I was three and a half, and I had been screaming for someone to pick me up ever since. I had to pick myself up, not in resentment, but by finding true empowerment. When Dad forced me into the Hoffman Process,[10] I awakened to the fact that everyone has wounds, not just me, and if we don't do the healing, anger and resentment start killing us. Learning to pick myself up and heal myself was what meditation and yoga and my quest for healers and psychics were all about.*

Saint Bill: Marcia, you understand so much more than I did, which means you won't die at 65 with unresolved anger and sadness eating away at you. You will become a living light and awaken others to healing.

Marcia: I'm far from that, Dad, but thanks for finally having faith in me and seeing how the suffering I've been able to resolve might at least help the people around me or who read my book or see my film. After you died, I met my meditation teacher Gary Springfield and have been meditating with him

---

[10] Founded in 1967 by Bob Hoffman, the Hoffman Process helps people become conscious of unconscious childhood conditioning.

for 16 years, watching him shed the ego to become the living light. He has shown me how to go inside the painful memories and process the wounded little girl playing out our old issues, as if you were still alive, but because you are dead, I keep reacting to other powerful men as if I'm still the little wounded girl with no voice.

For example, there are screams of powerlessness still inside my cells when I see my *Bardo Blues* film trailer go to number three on most-viewed trailers, with Disney and Pixar films at the 1 and 2 spot. We paid nothing, so this is organic authentic views, but today it's #9 because Star Wars came out. I feel powerless, but then I catch myself. It is always up and down, Dad, and besides, how do you compete with big male-driven Hollywood institutions, anyway? Indy films are no longer valued, so why not start my own self-sustaining studio? You did that for me, Dad: thinking outside the box.

Thanks to Gary, I can now pick up that little girl and love her and bring the light of God into her. Or memories of you yelling in your office and calling me names over the lawsuit after my show went off the air, or the letter you sent me about giving up on my dream just because I asked you for some American miles so I could travel to a meeting in London. Like getting into debt, Dad—you said I wasn't going to make money being an artist, and so far you've been right. But my powerlessness over not being heard is changing. Such memories no longer run like tape loops in my head. For years, I stuffed them deep in my cells and kept eating sugar, smoking pot, and drinking alcohol to keep them from coming out in one long scream like that painting by Edvard Munch. Everything dark can be alchemized into light, Dad, I know that now.

Saint Bill: I was so wrong, Marcia. Here, the only thing that means anything is intention and working to help people with their good intentions.

Marcia: You did that for many while on the Earth, Dad—just not for me.

Saint Bill (shaking his head): No, Marcia, most of what I did for others wasn't about them so much as it was about me. What you are doing that I didn't do is you are learning to validate yourself just by being who you are. It has nothing to do with the outside world validating you.

Marcia: Not necessarily, Dad. I want that brass ring of validation as an artist and am still pursuing it. What is different is I'm not going to allow my uncertainties and fears to destroy me, even if all of New York and Hollywood decide I'm a failure. I will never again view myself that way. And when you were dying but didn't know it, that letter about giving up on my dream and you wouldn't emotionally or financially support me anymore—that letter killed me. I almost lost my mind. I screamed and cried when I learned you only had a few days left and had given the order not to let me into the hospital room due to the stress of my director's lawsuit. I deeply regret your being named in that lawsuit, Dad; he probably thought you would pay rather than go through public humiliation. I hadn't been able to pay him after I'd paid the crew . . .

Saint Bill: Bygones, Marcia, bygones. But we were still able to say goodbye. (*Laughter.*) With all the tubes and sedatives, I no longer looked like a movie star, did I?

Marcia (*tearfully*): As I held your shaking hand, I realized you knew it was the end and were trying to tell me how sorry you were.

Saint Bill: And now we're talking—the dead and the living—and healing is happening.

*I suddenly understood that some people are awakened to who they are by love, but most people awaken through suffering, the path my father and I had had to tread. He had changed the hotel industry for the better, given tons of money away, started research on depression and meditation at Stanford University, set up a foundation to help those with mental illness, was generous with employees, friends and family, all while working out his childhood wounds that had almost destroyed him. I was doing the same but with the*

165

*advantage of more hindsight, and I had not abandoned my daughter.*

Marcia: I couldn't get one man in Hollywood to back my projects, nor could I move to LA with my daughter living in San Francisco. I couldn't abandon her like I'd been abandoned—you understand that, don't you, Dad?

Saint Bill: Yes, Marcia.

Marcia: So while watching me go broke, you feared the worst for my inheritance, didn't you? Is that why you changed your will on my birthday and didn't tell me?

Saint Bill: I was trying to make sure you didn't go through all the money, Marcia, given how poor you were at managing money.

Marcia: So you left me with the worst trustees on the planet—the most manipulative, sexist men possible?

Saint Bill: My shadow did that, Marcia. They were controlling men like me, good at serving the company and themselves but not at serving you and my granddaughter.

Marcia: And when I sued them because they were hardly giving me any money and had already drained the trust of a million dollars because they could, I still couldn't get them removed. I wouldn't have a tax lien today if you hadn't chosen those vultures.

Saint Bill: And yet most people can't say they've self-financed an entire movie like you have, right, Marcia? Think of that.

Marcia: True, but without the trust money, I couldn't have done the film, Dad. Remember how much you loved the academy awards? I dream of getting an academy award. This film won't get it, but maybe it will get a nomination. I'm betting the next one will. But who cares about awards? My dream is for people to see *Bardo Blues* and learn that we never die, that we are eternal, and that healing our karma in this life means we won't have to keep dragging it into other lives, right, Dad?

Saint Bill: Exactly, Marcia. (*Laughter.*) I'll probably have to return as a woman to experience how sexist I've been as a man and how I didn't give my daughter a fair shake unless she did what I decided she should do. Mea culpa, Marcia. But I was taught you have to go by the rules, which you never did.

Marcia: You didn't go by the rules either, Dad, so why was I supposed to? Just because I'm female? You almost went broke with your first two hotels, and you were broke most of the time you were married to Mom while making inventions you couldn't sell. Remember the hotdog cooker before its time? A few years later, it became a hit!

Saint Bill: That's true. And friends' money, along with the bank, gave me more time to pull off the first two hotels.

Marcia: After you died, your best friend said you and I were similar in how we both took risks for our visions. The difference was that you'd already worked hard in investment banking to make the money you needed for your big risk, but only after the failures during my childhood. Dad, remember when I first got on TV and was new to San Francisco and had no one to share my special moment with, so I decided to come up to your house in St. Helena—

Saint Bill: Yes, I regret that moment.

Marcia: How do you even know what I'm going to say?

Saint Bill: We review our lives when we die, Marcia, and that moment came up loud and clear.

Marcia: I'll never forget it. In fact, it feels like it happened yesterday. It took me ten years to get over it.

Saint Bill: I basically took your special moment of achieving a life goal and knocked you down. Threw a punch right into your solar plexus.

Marcia: I was so depressed, especially when you played golf at the AT&T
tournament when I finally got on national TV in 1996, thanks to Dick Clark. Maybe in my unconscious I believed I would

never be successful because you didn't think I would, like your stepfather almost did to you.

Saint Bill: I watched a lot of your TV segments on Fridays at home.

Marcia: But still I got no validation for how hard I was working to make money. When I tried so hard in the entertainment business and didn't get a break—*Rock'n'Roll Evening News* in '86, *Video Dreamers* in '88, and all the rest—you thought I should give up. Even that letter to me while you were dying in March 2001 was about giving up. When I finally got on TV, your Fox GM 'friend'—the guy you got into the exclusive golf club—only let me on the air two minutes per week and paid me $150 per segment because, he said, my daddy was rich. Beyond the golf club membership, all he wanted from me was another notch on his belt. The interview dinner with him wasn't a professional interview at all—

Saint Bill: I believed him and not you. Not my finest hour.

Marcia: Maybe my first late night show wasn't great, Dad, but at least I didn't have sex with the GM to get it on the air.

Saint Bill: We're all connected, Marcia. We're all God playing different parts in the drama called life. If we learn not to identify with our masks, we have a chance at seeing God shine right through the Earth Bardo. If we identify with the mask, then we run the risk of remaining a victim and dragging old wounds around with us, blaming others, then dying and dragging them into a rerun life. It's energetic patterns that make people play pre-determined parts.

Marcia: On the whole, Dad, I have to admit that you did me a favor by playing the role that made me suffer, but in the end, Dad, is it all just a dream, an illusion like the Buddhists say it is?

Saint Bill (*smiles*): Yes, it's a movie, Marcia. You and I love movies. Only in this Bardo movie, you're not the director. (*Winks.*) I was so consumed with my own life that I was unaware of the pivotal role I played in your life until I woke up after death. Because I was incapable of loving myself, I couldn't love you and therefore couldn't see you. That's how it works. Once we stop emotionally reacting to the movie and pay attention to how it works, we can change the script, heal the wounds, and transmute darkness into light. Spiritual masters transition into heaven because their spiritual bodies are light, whereas most of us drag darkness with us from cradle to grave, fighting death, and then taking up a new life to confront the same darkness again but in a different scene . . .

*As I listened, I thought about how the desire for fame had driven me since I was 12 years old. Part of it was how deeply I felt destined to share my creativity and love of performing, but another part was about how my father would finally notice me if I was famous. Was that why fame had eluded me? Certainly, my father had never truly seen who I was, but does anyone ever truly see who others are?*

Saint Bill: Death is painful and frightening because we resist healing our darkest and deepest of wounds. In the after-death Bardo, we encounter everything and everyone we affected on Earth and have the opportunity to accept and forgive ourselves and other actors in the movie that was our life. The afterlife is an opportunity for more learning. If we can't fully awaken and transmute our consciousness, we'll eventually pick parents and prepare for a new movie. Our old relationships and unresolved wounds will begin to vibrate and draw the life situations we need for yet another Earth Bardo opportunity for healing. You picked me, Marcia, to teach you what powerlessness feels like, so I took your power and refused to empower you. Thus you had to learn self-empowerment from a position of powerlessness. No one is really a victim, Marcia, but we may play the victim until we can forgive everyone involved and everything that has happened, once we realize that the plot of our movie was all about something we needed to learn. If we take full responsibility for the movie, then we begin to learn how to

169

create, not just react, and awaken to the consciousness that we chose it all. This Earth Bardo may seem crazy and violent and painful, but it is sacred and not just an illusion, because it is here that we actually learn to love and forgive ourselves and others . . .

Saint Bill's voice began to fade. I closed my eyes—or was I opening them? It all felt kind of like an acid trip, which, by the way, I have only done twice. Everything on Earth has a correspondence in the spiritual world, Swedenborg said, and our eyes and ears see and hear the spiritual before the physical. Everything here is there, just as Hermes Trismegistus, the thrice-great Hermes, said: *As above, so below.*

Remarkable.

# Conclusion

This book must accompany the *Bardo Blues* launch. The PR firm is struggling to get me and the story I have to tell noticed in a time when everything is a one-liner, and if you're not famous or infamous, it's almost impossible to get a headline. Not to mention that no one wants to hear about transcendence or spirituality, nor about understanding and curing mental illness because my brother suffered from it.

But this is the year that female directors (and the lack thereof) are finally being noticed by the 4 Percent Challenge. USC Annenberg asked the entertainment industry to help women directors, and now my Big Pharma corruption script I have been writing with my partner Brian Gross (who plays the brother in *Bardo Blues*) is going out to major female actors, thanks to Jane Fonda's interest and the help of her agent. Ten percent of *Bardo Blues* receipts goes to onemind.org that has raised $220 million for researching healthy and unhealthy brains, set up a suicide and depression line at UCLA, and gotten Ken Burns to do a documentary on mental illness.

I am Bill Kimpton's daughter, one of the heirs to the Kimpton Hotels. I am also the unknown woman who produced, wrote, directed, acted, did the props, makeup and costumes in a foreign country with a crew of 12 American and 4 Thai and all pre-production and all post-production without an assistant. Without Justin McAleece and Jason Shamai, I couldn't have done it. Do you know three people who have done an entire film on their own? So far, no news outlets are interested in covering how hard it is for women in film to get financial backing so that they're not doing everything themselves—even in the year of the 4 Percent Challenge!

My good friend Kat has started Beneficial Bank to make sure banks are good, clean, and not corrupt. She called her new friend Jane Fonda to tell her about how serious I am about taking Big Pharma down. Jane wrote me a personal note saying, "Let's take it down."

I cried when I read her email.

While I was skiing down the only run on three mountains that my brother and I skied together, I had the idea of holding up the *Bardo Blues* poster when the film launches May 3rd, to fight mental illness or at least make others remember that May is mental illness awareness month. Where did this idea come from on our favorite run? Graham? my Higher Self? What is it that takes form as a movie, painting, photo, music?

Two weeks later, Jane sent me a photo of herself and the *Bardo Blues* poster with the email subject line: Jane holding poster. The picture said it all. The 82-year-old still beautiful drama and comedy actress, academy award winning actor and producer, activist for the voiceless and marginalized, was holding the poster for my film, because she wants to find a cure for mental illness and maybe she saw and loved my movie. Like my brother, her mother had started off great but had descended into the madness or hell of a mind gone awry. It almost happened to me and it surely almost happened to Jane if you read between the lines of the documentary she directed and starred in, Jane Fonda in Five Acts.[11]

So why do some maintain a healthy mind under duress (or at least keep unhealth at bay) while others slip over the edge? Some survive trauma, tragedy, abandonment, drugs and alcohol, and others—usually the more sensitive and less "resilient"—end up killing themselves one way or another. The son of Brandon Staglin, founder of onemind.org, has schizo-

---

[11] *https://www.hbo.com/documentaries/jane-fonda-in-five-acts.*

phrenia. How could my brother produce 60 great pieces of artwork and not survive? In honor of Jane's mother and my brother, Jane holds the poster of *Bardo Blues* a month before launch.

Jane Fonda has been a role model for me ever since her 1978 film Coming Home. I haven't met her and hope to, but when I tell people about how this Hollywood icon, artist, and activist is supporting my first movie to come out to the public since my late night show went off the air in 1998, I get mixed reactions. Most women love her for her remarkable accomplishments while others refuse to forget Hanoi Jane, no matter how many times she asks for forgiveness. She was young and opposed to war and war crimes in an incendiary era. People may choose to see her act of defiance as a betrayal, but I choose to see the courage it took to stand up against war.

To think Jane Fonda has stepped forward in her crone years to help my movie is nothing short of a remarkable ending to a remarkable story. Movies that help humanity and change consciousness in an era of voyeur "reality" TV? What a concept.

How does one get out of any Bardo, and in my case the Hollywood Bardo? Quit the entire scene? See through one illusion after another?

In writing this book, I've really struggled. Just as when we die, I've had to go back into my life and review it. If Bardo is a state of mind . . . According to the Tibetan Book of the Dead and Swedenborg, at death the world of spirits—angels, your Higher Self, God, relatives who've made the jump beyond light speed—meets you as your unique spirit lifts out of the body to be re-united off-Earth with its original divine self. If this is true, then why not do your life review here while still in the body? Why not alchemize each emotional experience stored in the cells that have been recording your history in this lifetime and possibly many previous lifetimes?

173

Gary Springfield described karma as "that which isn't loved." So if we are only a particle-wave energy field of light and dark, then our task is surely to alchemize the dark fully into the light. If we were able in one lifetime to love all things and beings to ourselves, then we could transmute our cells storing the darkness of each emotional experience in a process that developmental biologist Bruce Lipton calls epigenetics. Imagine doing a conscious epigenetic life review while still alive so nothing of darkness is held over for the next lifetime?

The true "memoir" may be just that creative and powerful: By observing the life tableau as exactly as possible with love, without re-living or re-traumatizing the 5-year-old or 35-year-old but just putting it down on the written page, we are changed.

The only reason I am doing this book and forcing myself to review my life is to inspire others to do the same. If I am no longer reliving the past or the past is no longer reliving itself, then the memories locked in my cells can be transformed and become that much more joy and happiness.

The self-defeating life patterns I've identified in this book are abandonment, powerlessness, and entrapment. When they "happened" to me over and over in the entertainment business, with men, and/or in other aspects of my life, I remained a helpless victim until I could recognize the pattern and make it conscious. Making it conscious changes the frequency. Meditation and yoga offered the daily practice of the presence of the light of consciousness that I needed in order to clear the darkness of repeated trauma patterns.

I used to let life just happen to me instead of moving hell and high water to learn how to conduct my life with pure intention and meaningful manifestation. I assumed that being born a superstar meant that if I was willing to work hard, I would become hugely famous with a lot of money and a wonderful family, and that I would spread light and love with every creative project I touched. The life I got wasn't the life I had imagined, but it was the life I had unconsciously created in order to learn exactly what I'm writing in this conclusion.

From among the many experiences that every life presents from its mixed-review banquet, it is suffering that has guided me the most, pushing me toward prioritizing finding the light of my soul so I have the right tools with which to transmute the darkness I most assuredly have encountered in the Bardo I found myself in. Transcending suffering is not about ignoring what can't be fixed, chanting it away, subscribing to the adage that "The past is in the past," etc. It is about learning to be a light while we are here on our darkened planet loaded with ongoing karma. It is about preparing to be a light in whatever dimensions we will enter after the death of the body.

If we are really just frequencies and waves of consciousness, what consciousness do we want to experience or work on for the brief time we are here? Most of humanity wants peace and happiness, but neither comes easy, given the many Bardo illusions to be waded through. We must first make our way through the karma of what we've created in past lives now embedded and disguised in situational dramas that begin to reveal themselves in childhood. Once we see through the new costumes and scenes, we can begin the work of removing the fixed, repetitive constellations of consciousness preventing our ongoing evolution.

This book was not about reliving every painful memory but uncovering the spiritual meaning (and hopefully humor) in the revelations. I found a wonderful editor I feared I might lose if I didn't keep up with facing what I had to face in order to write the book I needed to write. People spend years writing books, but I wanted this book out when *Bardo Blues* launched. I love creating movies in every aspect, from writing the screenplay, producing the locations and casting the actors, to directing the vision and even acting roles I write. My favorite aspect is editing the film and seeing my final vision come into focus and fruition. I loved hosting and producing my own comedy rock'n'roll shows and interviewing interesting guests. I do not love writing a book. If it isn't dialogue for a movie I'll get to see and create the visuals for, writing is not fun, other than now and then getting on a roll laughing about how absurd some life experiences were, particularly from a distance.

The looming May 3 deadline drove me in and out of old habits, including drinking. I had quit for the 100th time. Hard writing in the morning, two drinks at lunch, then editing and rewriting in the afternoon fueled by the two drinks. But evenings of reliving what I was exorcising on the written page now and then meant a lot more drinks. I thought I was in the acceptance phase, but all I was doing was re-traumatizing myself as I wrote, instead of staying in my happy, productive screenplay writer persona enjoying marketing my upcoming movie.

I am, for the most part, really happy, but I definitely haven't been smiling during this last phase of the book life review. I've kept getting stuck in the Hollywood Bardo like one long refrain: If I had all this talent, why didn't I get to live as a working successful artist? Why didn't Hollywood allow a woman in late night when I was that woman? Why wasn't I with a loving man? Why did my ex-husband put me through hell, and why did our daughter get so gravely ill? Etc.

Now, the form of the life review memoir is complete. I've learned not to re-traumatize myself by reliving each experience but to instead observe how the experience taught me more about becoming a living, breathing bit of light on Earth. With the insights that arose through this process, I will now be more aware of ruses from within or without to draw me back into a Bardo state, including my own resistance to acceptance. If I find myself heading toward a mind hell or downward emotional spiral, I will know more about how to exit the hell of the moment so as to remain in the heaven of the moment (as long as I'm not calling AT&T).

Imagine what a world it would be if each of us could do this consistently.

Remember and release all darkness for this lifetime, past lifetimes, and even lifetimes going forward. I release the darkness from out of my cells and body. We are here to discover the truth and radiate joy. There is so much to enjoy, live, and experience in our short miraculous time on planet Earth, however many Bardos attempt to mislead us and keep us buried in the past.

*Before enlightenment, chop wood, carry water. After enlightenment, chop wood, carry water.*

Do the inner work of the life review and be prepared to be surprised.

Made in the USA
San Bernardino, CA
29 April 2019